Critical Perspectives on African Genocide

Critical Perspectives on African Genocide

Memory, Silence, and Anti-Black Political Violence

Edited by
Alfred Frankowski, Jeanine Ntihirageza,
and Chielozona Eze

ROWMAN & LITTLEFIELD
Lanham • Boulder • New York • London

Published by Rowman & Littlefield
An imprint of The Rowman & Littlefield Publishing Group, Inc.
4501 Forbes Boulevard, Suite 200, Lanham, Maryland 20706
www.rowman.com

6 Tinworth Street, London, SE11 5AL, United Kingdom

Copyright © 2021 by Alfred Frankowski, Jeanine Ntihirageza, and Chielozona Eze
Copyright in individual chapters is held by the respective chapter authors.

All rights reserved. No part of this book may be reproduced in any form or by any electronic or mechanical means, including information storage and retrieval systems, without written permission from the publisher, except by a reviewer who may quote passages in a review.

British Library Cataloguing in Publication Information Available

Library of Congress Cataloging-in-Publication Data

Names: Frankowski, Alfred, editor. | Ntihirageza, Jeanine, 1961– editor. | Eze, Chielozona, editor.
Title: Critical perspectives on African genocide : memory, silence, and anti-Black political violence / edited by Alfred Frankowski, Jeanine Ntihirageza, Chielozona Eze.
Description: Lanham : Rowman & Littlefield, [2021] | Includes bibliographical references and index. | Summary: "This text explores critical perspectives on the intersections between colonialism, political violence, and environmentalism to deepen our understanding of genocide and genocidal violence."—Provided by publisher.
Identifiers: LCCN 2020045779 (print) | LCCN 2020045780 (ebook) | ISBN 9781538147030 (cloth) | ISBN 9781538150016 (epub) | ISBN 9781538150337 (pbk)
Subjects: LCSH: Genocide—Africa—History. | Political violence—Africa—History. | Genocide survivors—Africa—Social conditions.
Classification: LCC DT30.5 .C76 2021 (print) | LCC DT30.5 (ebook) | DDC 364.151096—dc23
LC record available at https://lccn.loc.gov/2020045779
LC ebook record available at https://lccn.loc.gov/2020045780

Contents

Acknowledgments   vii

Introduction   ix
Alfred Frankowski, Jeanine Ntihirageza, and Chielozona Eze

1   Burundi 1972: Remembering a Forgotten Genocide   1
  René Lemarchand

2   *Repenser pour mieux panser* (Remembering for Better Healing):
  A Survivor's Account of the 1972 Burundi Genocide   13
  Jeanine Ntihirageza

3   Anti-Imperialist Rhetoric and Patterns of Genocide Denial in
  Zimbabwe   27
  Chielozona Eze

4   American Slavery, the New Jim Crow, and Genocide   39
  Lissa Skitolsky

5   The "Post-Conflict State" in Africa: Challenging the Continued
  Normalization of Genocidal Violence   55
  Patricia Daley

6   Hermeneutical Aesthetics, Commemoration, and Mourning
  in Post-Genocide Rwanda   75
  Alfred Frankowski

7   Environmental Racism as Genocide: A Case Study of Shell
  Bluff, Georgia   95
  Milanika S. Turner

Index 111

List of Contributors 117

Acknowledgments

This book came out of the Rethinking Genocide in Africa and the African Diaspora symposia, held at Northeastern Illinois University from 2014 to 2017. During those years, the Genocide Research Group, a collective of interdisciplinary genocide scholars, held symposia that focused on genocide within Africa and genocide as a category of violence against peoples of the African diaspora. Our symposia focused on remembrance and silence, gender and violence, and intervention, culture and morality, and always contained much more.

We want to extend a special thank you to the Northeastern Illinois University (NEIU) community. First, we would like to acknowledge the support of Dr. Larry Frank, for his unwavering support of African teaching and research at NEIU. Second, we owe our gratitude to Dr. Wamucii Njogu for her considerable encouragement and wholehearted guidance. Third, we would like to thank the faculty at Northeastern Illinois University in the departments of Anthropology, English, English Language Program, Teaching English to Speakers of Other Languages, Philosophy, Justice Studies, and especially to African and African American Studies. In particular, we would like to thank Teddy Bofman, John Casey, Courtney Francis, Stacey Gougen, Sarah Hoagland, Tim Libretti, Dan Milsky, Sophia Mihic, Kristen Over, TK Okoson, Ryan Poll, William Stone, Cris Tofolo, and Gina Wells among so many others. We would like to acknowledge the work of Sarah Travis and all of the students who attended the symposiums over the years. The real legacy of this work lies with how they will generate the next generation of questions for the field of genocide studies.

We would like to the editors at Rowman & Littlefield International, especially Frankie Mace, for supporting this project from the start, and Scarlet Furness, for providing guidance and support throughout the editorial and production process. We would like to thank Kristen Hedberg, Elisa von Joeden Forgey, Donald Bloxham, Anne O'Byrne, Martin Schuster, George Yancy, Falguni Sheth, Marianna Ortega, Kris Sealy, Kenneth Stikkers, and Anthony Steinbock for their support, advice, and mentorship. We would also like to thank the work of the anonymous reviewers for this project. Last but not least, we want to acknowledge our family and friends, both near and far, past and present.

Introduction

Alfred Frankowski, Jeanine Ntihirageza, and Chielozona Eze

Every continent has some experience with genocide. The word itself provokes one to think of the extreme horrors of political violence from the past, or to imagine conditions under which a state of war has broken into a brute state of mass killing, or consider where extremist ideology has been carried over to the extremes of ethnic cleansing. What is missing in this way of thinking about genocide is that it *is* part of, and continuous with, the actions of nations. It is something that happens in the building and governing of states and nations, rather than what happens only in the breakdown of a society or the abnormal condition of politics. As historian and genocide scholar, Mark Levene has stated, "Genocide is not fixed in the make-up of regimes. But it is something that *different* types of regimes *do*."[1] Whether genocide takes place in Germany, Bosnia, or Rwanda, it describes the action of putting the political violence experienced by citizens within a context where its realization is also its legitimation. What we think of as a break with, or breaking down of society through the employment of genocidal violence, is a nation proceeding in contradiction with itself.

The contradiction that genocidal violence lays bare is already always apparent in the limits of genocide discourse. These limits should concern us at a global level because of how they naturalize this form of contradiction against the legibility of lives and deaths as a result of this political violence. Indeed, what makes something legible as genocide matters as much as the way we problematize (or fail to problematize) the contradictions of a nation's violence.[2] In all cases where genocide is an open question for analysis, we see the tactics of the denial, erasure, and forgetting employed as explicit methods of silencing. Beyond this, however, within genocide discourse itself, the context of the analysis is usually shifted to two pragmatic questions: what do we do now to reconcile the conflict and how do we prevent it from happening again? The shift to these questions presupposes a situation in which a recognition of genocidal violence is framing the public discourse and critically informing the genocide discourse. This is exactly what is denied in most cases where the state situation that created the conditions for genocide continues—and it is what perpetuates silence, social amnesia, and the continuance of normative political violence, even after genocide has been accepted.

Nowhere is genocide more complexly situated to attempt to meet these challenges than in Africa and the African diaspora, placed as they are within the history of colonialism and the residue of its violence as well as the explicit and implicit methods of silence that make it illegible. As Dirk Moses argues, "Colonial and imperial wars are not usually considered genocidal. Once regions are 'pacified'—that is, armed resistance is broken—the occupiers settle down to the business of governing."[3] Silence, memory, and the residue of political violence are always an issue to be grappled with after genocide, but they are taken up and continued as power dynamics specifically in the contexts of colonization, and that is nowhere more present than in the cases of African genocide, and under-theorized in the existing literature.

The power dynamics of silence, memory, and displacement are tools for denying or obscuring genocide. But they are particularly potent when they are expressions of anti-black political violence. Everything hangs upon the framework of the genocide discourse itself and its ability to critically engage its own contradictions. Genocide discourse depends on the recognition that the powerful acknowledge the rights of the disempowered and the abuse of these rights by the powerful themselves—and more. It requires the recognition of the humanity of the dehumanized by the institutions that enabled those who committed the dehumanization—and more. It depends on each context of genocide learning to hear, see, and think the injustice from which the state violence sprung and continues even after the genocide, and on reframing how to hear the screams of the dead as a continual condition through which those past screams continue to be the transfigured cries for a just world that lays before us as an open question.

Critical Perspectives on African Genocide, approaches genocide from the standpoint of Africa and the African diaspora. The context of the essays here is critically focused on the political and cultural intersections that stem from the colonization of Africa, of Africans, and the African diaspora. This volume originated from a recognition that there was a dearth of literature on forms of genocide against African forms of genocide in the people of African descent in the West. Genocide in Africa has received only fleeting attention; and this has not only served to create a vacuum of knowledge but also compounded the problem of how and in what ways complicity with genocide continues. There is a dearth of literature on specifically African genocides. Genocide in

Zimbabwe, Uganda; against the Herero and Namaqua of South West Africa (1904 and 1907), and the Congo (1835–1909) (which might be the deadliest genocide in twentieth-century history) are almost completely absent from international discourse and genocide research.[4] The problem is more far reaching than simply which genocides have and have not been studied. The problem is that even in the acknowledgement that this is an under-theorized, under-researched area of study, the field proceeds without asking how and in what way the study of genocide itself plays a role in promoting the general silence on genocide within African contexts.

The essays in this volume do not simply claim that there is not enough literature on genocides in or against African peoples. They start their thinking from African contexts in order to expand the discourse, conceptualization, and critical tools forged within genocide research. While the literature on genocide in the context of Africa and against peoples of the African diaspora is growing, it remains clear that it is still rarely considered more than a source of comparative analysis. Genocide against African people in the diaspora has been only a topical area of research within genocide studies but, up to this point, there have been no academic volumes that collect together scholars working exclusively within the area of African or Black genocide studies, there are no academic departments or programs in the United States that currently recognize research into genocide with a focus on anti-black violence as a specialization, there are no academic forums that focus on genocide in Africa and the diaspora,[5] and there are no professional journals to support research exclusively on genocide in Africa and African contexts, outside of individual research articles and the occasional special issue.[6] Bringing Africa into the discourse on genocide has rarely framed the mass death of blacks as being more than an unfortunate result of modernity; never has a genocide against blacks resulted in a critical shift of the discourse on genocide.

We are arguing not only that genocide against Africans and people of African descent has been denied, forgotten, or hidden but also that the framework of genocide has not yet developed in a way that would allow for recognition and adequate critical attention toward such forms of genocide. Even in the case of the Rwandan Genocide against the Tutsi, from the UN to individual scholars, it has often been discussed as an example of the international community's failure to act and its subsequent guilt from inaction. Titles such as *The International Response to Conflict and Genocide: Lessons from the Rwanda Experience* and *The Role of the International Community in the Rwandan Genocide* and the like, point to a self-serving superficial exchange of views about this genocide, not an African genocide committed in the context of Africa and part of the African experience in any real or unique sense. To the world, the Rwandan Genocide against the Tutsi is not African, it is international, thus removing a bottom up political and sociocultural approach to understanding this atrocity.

For us and for future generations, the question of genocide shifts toward understanding how the dynamics of oppression are intertwined with questions of genocide, especially in contexts of global black political violence. In order to accord the voice of the oppressed a deserved attention, there needs to be some form of legitimate space where such voices can occupy the center, rather than continue to be relegated to the margins. This volume provides such a space by examining the uniqueness of the global situation of Africans and the globally black in regard to genocide.

Furthermore, with this volume, we draw together voices within Africa and the diaspora in critical ways to develop the questions around how we conceive of political violence, in general, and anti-black violence, in particular, as a global pattern of genocide. We believe the volume is long overdue in the field of genocide studies and will add much to the general discourse—and mean much to those whose voices and experiences have only received marginal attention, if not complete silence up to this point.

CRITICAL FRAMEWORK

Critical Perspectives on African Genocide focuses on the development of a variety of frameworks through which we can think more critically about violence stemming from genocide within African and anti-black contexts. The critical framework each of the essays start from is that genocide describes a pattern of political violence embedded in the epistemic, aesthetic, social, and historical elements of a political culture. As the sociologist Orlando Patterson and the feminist political philosopher Claudia Card have both argued, genocide is not simply reducible to mass killing; it is a process that takes root in forms of social death, regardless of the number of people physically killed.[7] Genocide is embedded in the social processes that cut groups off from their traditions, family, and cultural life. With this shared critical framework in mind, memory, silence, and anti-black political violence are explored within the various essays in this text.

Genocide itself is historically ancient, but conceptually modern. The term, "genocide," which was coined by the Polish jurist, historian, and legal scholar, Raphaël Lemkin, was meant to provide a critical framework in which to think the coordinated violence perpetuated against groups. By bringing together *genos* and *cide,* he sought to emphasize the perpetuation of violence on a group, on the one hand, and how this ought to require international response, on the other. Moreover, his influence was paramount in how it shaped Article 2 of the United Nations Convention on the Prevention and Punishment of the Crime of Genocide (1948). Within this context, the UN defines the legal concept of genocide as

> any of the following acts committed with intent to destroy, in whole or in part, a national, ethnical, racial or religious group, as such: killing members of the group; causing serious bodily or mental harm to members of the group; deliberately inflicting on the group conditions of life calculated to bring about its physical destruction in whole or in part; imposing measures intended to prevent births within the group; [and] forcibly transferring children of the group to another group.[8]

The UN's definition is broad and based in large part on the work of Lemkin's *Axis Rule in Occupied Europe*.[9] Lemkin argues that the purpose of such a broad classification is to outline a social and political phenomenon, one that involves multiple ways in which state violence is mobilized or perpetuated against a class, gender, or race of people.[10] In addition, Lemkin's work remains important in how the word "genocide," itself calls into question the political violence that stems from the contexts of colonialism, both in the expanse of Europe and the fracturing of Africa.[11] For this reason, his work remains a distinguished model for contemporary genocide research beyond the way the term is legally defined.

The definition of genocide is one thing, but the way it has been used to identify the legitimacy of the state and national forms of violence that contradict a group's legitimacy, and the group's claim to life, is quite another. Both require critical framing of the situation and the critique of the standards of legitimacy itself. This is illustrated in the *We Charge Genocide* petition, of 1951, where African Americans formed the first group to charge a country with genocide. The Civil Rights Council (CRC), which was a group of legal scholars and activists, submitted the petition to the UN offices in both New York and Paris. The nearly 200-page document outlined and supported the case that the United States fulfilled every clause of the UN definition of genocide. They provided a copious amount of information that collected accounts of discrimination, police brutality, abduction, false imprisonment, torture, and lynching. The CRC wrote,

> The genocide of which we complain is as much a fact as gravity. The whole world knows of it. The proof is in every day's newspapers, in every one's sight and hearing in these United States ... Its very familiarity disguises its horror. It is a crime so embedded in law, so explained away by specious rationale, so hidden by talk of liberty, that even the conscience of the tender minded is

sometimes dulled. Yet the conscience of mankind cannot be beguiled from its duty by the pious phrases and the deadly legal euphemisms with which its perpetrators seek to transform their guilt into high moral purpose.[12]

And further,

We speak, too, as world citizens, certain that if the forces of predatory reaction are allowed to continue their present policies, are allowed to continue a profitable genocide against Americans, the time will not be long removed, the world being what it is, that the same forces will practice genocide on a wider scale against nationals and other nations. So we plead not for ourselves alone but for all mankind.[13]

While the CRC's employment of the term "genocide" directs attention to the coordination of forms of state violence mobilized toward particular groups as a normative injustice lived, the *We Charge Genocide* petition was dismissed primarily *because* of its use of the term "genocide."[14] This was not the result of a wayward society or a lack of moral integrity, nor was it a lack of knowledge or insight. Rather, the application of critical erudition of the law and of history, of politics and of culture was mobilized to deny the legitimacy of the charge, regardless of what the document said.[15] Moreover, the petition still remains one in which the claims, no matter whether they are accepted or rejected, are routinely taken up, whether critically or uncritically, as making no claim on the field of genocide studies or genocide research itself. Rather, it remains complicit with the contradictions of state violence through the illegibility of state processes that ensure the unjust deaths of blacks in America. Rather than prompt a critical turn toward the conditions of legitimacy of genocide research, the rejection of the petition itself has prompted genocide scholars to clarify the difference between discrimination and genocide and between the institution of slavery and concentration camps during the Holocaust.[16]

Recently, the Black Lives Matter social justice movement and international protests in response to the police homicide of several black men and women, underscore a deep pattern of lethal violence within police departments across the country. This development calls for more attention to be paid to not only the human rights violations that may be being committed daily but indeed also the stealth genocide on black people to the degree that it is designed to instill terror in them and suppress their political agency. Up to this point, however, international recognition has not critically framed the violence directed against blacks in the United States as human rights violations, and still has not accepted this situation as a form of genocide. Because of this, we question the way genocide has become a critical framework through which one can see or analyze state violence.[17] We acknowledge that the UN definition has become almost a roadblock to the interpretation of other cases of genocide in the world, particularly in Africa and the diaspora.[18] It is through the distinction itself and maybe even as part of the employment of a critical approach to genocide that Africa and the diaspora become reduced, minimized, if not altogether erased, unseen, or un-thought—or, at least unthought as something more than a part of a country's history.

By thematizing genocide in Africa, and anti-black political violence in the diaspora, we understand that, for some readers at least, we are moving into uncomfortable territory. We understand that the essays contained in this volume are provoking a discourse on state violence and forms of anti-black social death that challenge the European assumptions of genocide or require different orientations toward the term "genocide" altogether. However, throughout this volume, there is a shared working out of the patterns of genocide as anti-black violence across the diaspora, and a challenge to think of just this relation as a critical framework for present and future analytical tools. Genocide within African contexts requires something extra for us to realize the impact and development of genocide; it requires that we read in and through the ramifications of what we know as genocide, but that we inquire into how we know it and what this knowing and unknowing means. It requires seeking a framework through which the legibility of systems of violence that continues irregularly, or illegibly, can be seen as genocidal violence. In order to achieve this, the contributions in this volume are attempting to strike at the intersections between colonialism, genocide, and anti-black political violence, and do so to provoke new ways of seeing and thinking of the urgency of global oppression. We are not calling attention to a globally comparative condition, for neither the slave nor the masses of exterminated blacks globally are comparable.[19] We are calling for a critical framework through which the violence against the globally black can been seen and must be heard, legitimately, critically, and morally.

What we are faced with, and what this volume attempts to shed light on, is not simply the challenge of recognizing instances of genocide in Africa and the African diaspora, but also of confronting the concrete, material, anti-black political violence that the term "genocide" and the collective scholarship of genocide studies intended to bring under critical frameworks. We cannot stand for the dynamics of silence on this topic and the methods of complicity that delegitimate a focus on violence against the globally black. Our turn toward a way of framing genocide within the intersections of Africa and African diaspora and colonialism and anti-black political violence is a turn toward a re-envisioning of critical approaches to genocide itself.

ORGANIZATION OF THE TEXT

By focusing on select analyses of genocide in Africa and the African diaspora, the authors note that there is a shift in current understandings of this phenomenon. We examine this shift from multiple angles to provoke new questions as well as awaken dormant ones. Each author analyzes a specific event or set of circumstances found in Africa and the diaspora, by supplying an analysis where formerly there was none, challenging dogmas that obstruct nuances essential to thinking about the genocide, or developing new conceptual and practical frameworks for thinking and rethinking genocide.

The volume begins with a brief chapter that provides an overview of the way forgetting and memory make continual states of genocide disappear. In "Burundi 1972: Remembering a Forgotten Genocide," René Lemarchand focuses on how the forgotten genocide in Burundi has a continual impact on the region. He argues that forgotten genocides have lessons that we have not begun to reconcile as of yet, and he calls our attention to the need to remember the complexity of the genocide and its relation to current affairs in Burundi. He proposes that we need more interwoven notions of memory to come to terms completely with the unfinished genocides of Burundi and Rwanda.

In the second chapter, "*Repenser pour mieux panser* (Remembering for Better Healing): A Survivor's Account of the 1972 Burundi Genocide," Jeanine Ntihirageza explores the experience of how a forgotten genocide continues to inflict harm on the survivors. Her chapter is part memoir, and as a survivor of the 1972 Burundi genocide, she describes what it is like for the genocide's victims and survivors to be blamed for the crime, to be denied a way of mourning lost relatives, and how it feels to witness a political denial of the genocide effectively take place. Ntihirageza argues for the remembrance of the Burundi genocide not only as a way of challenging how this genocide has been ignored but also as a way of critically rethinking the present.

The third chapter explores how the charge of genocide is routinely silenced through tactics of denial, often making them illegible globally. In "Anti-Imperialist Rhetoric and Patterns of Genocide Denial in Zimbabwe," Chielozona Eze critically examines the way in which Robert Mugabe's dictatorship employed anti-colonial, anti-imperialist rhetoric as a means of genocide denial, constantly recasting the genocide of 20,000 people as casualties of war. The need to remember is constantly reframed as the need to forget. Eze offers a nuanced reading of the need not only to remember the past but also to see the face of the genocidaire in the language and texts that is denying its past. The rhetoric of the genocidaire shapes not only the way in which we regard the past but also what we misrecognize in the present.

The question of how genocide is denied is continued in the fourth chapter. In Lissa Skitolsky's, "American Slavery, the New Jim Crow, and Genocide" she argues that American slavery, Jim Crow, and mass incarceration of African Americans in the United States is a form of genocide that has not simply been forgotten, but that has continued without recognition. Against the currents in genocide studies largely, she argues for the expansion of genocidal categories to include slavery, Jim Crow, and the New Jim Crow. She argues that we need to frame these practices as genocide and explores how the intersections between abolitionist approaches to mass incarceration can be critically reshaped when they are combined with trauma informed politics.

Chapter 5 focuses on the role of the nation in reproducing genocidal violence after the most explicit forms of killing have died down. In "The 'Post-Conflict State' in Africa: Challenging the Continued Normalization of Genocidal Violence," Patricia Daley critiques the ways in which state-building, militarization, and perpetual conflict zones are contextualized in terms of peace-keeping efforts. She develops the concept of the genocidal state, especially its manifestations in the era of neoliberalism and in the emergence of the "post-conflict" state. She critically points out that African societies have struggled for alternative forms of state-building with difference, equity, and a common humanity at its core, and considers the intellectual challenges of promoting alternative ontologies and epistemologies to the hegemonic Western model.

As many of the other chapters lay out, memory is essential to post-genocide society. In the sixth chapter, "Hermeneutical Aesthetics, Commemoration, and Mourning in Post-Genocide Rwanda," Alfred Frankowski analyzes the two main forms of national commemoration, namely the sites of massacre and the National Mourning Plays. He traces how these forms of commemoration work as both forms of public memory and as methods that obscure the lived experience of the Rwandan genocide against the Tutsi, and against the colonial past that gave rise to the genocide itself. He argues that while genocide commemoration is necessary, commemoration is more complex, and more complexly rooted in the aesthetics of the political experience of the post-genocide.

The volume concludes with a focus on the intersection between activism and anti-black genocide. Milanika S. Turner's "Environmental Racism as Genocide: A Case Study of Shell Bluff, Georgia" explores the critical relationship between environmental crises and anti-black genocidal violence. In this essay, she critically explores the effects of anti-genocide activism against the backdrop of Shell Corporation's policy toward the environment in Shell Bluff, Georgia. Deriving inspiration from Rob Nixon's concept of slow violence,[20] Turner argues that environmental racism, as exemplified by Shell Bluff, is not only destructive to that particular environment but also, in effect, shortens the lifespans of the inhabitants and ultimately undermines the community's ability to flourish. She illustrates how this is particularly disastrous toward African Americans in that region and thus perpetuates a form of genocidal anti-black political violence.

All of the contributions in this volume hold that the critical analysis of genocide in Africa and the African diaspora requires that we draw into thinking that which evades being questioned, and as such, that we seek to contest those limits that particularize anti-black political violence. In this way, this project is necessarily incomplete, and the chapters contained herein are only the beginning of research that can and hopefully will inspire new directions in the field. Each chapter is an invitation to engage issues that must be developed at later times and within different environments. Our hope is that by making this thematic intervention, the voices of the oppressed are not only heard but also used to lay critical claim to those frameworks in which they have been and continue to be denied.

NOTES

1. Mark Levene, *Genocide in the Age of the Nation State, Vol. 1: The Meaning of Genocide* (New York, NY: I.B. Tauris, 2008), 41.

2. Douglas Irving-Erickson, Thomas La Pointe, and Alexander Hinton, "Introduction: Power, Knowledge, Memory," in *Hidden Genocides: Power, Knowledge, Memory*, ed. A. Hinton, T. La Pointe, and D. Irvin-Erickson (New Brunswick, NJ: Rutgers University Press, 2014), 1–17.

3. A. Dirk Moses, "Empire, Colony, and Genocide: Key Terms and the Philosophy of History," in *Empire, Colony, Genocide: Conquest, Occupation, and Subaltern Resistance in World History*, ed. D. Moses (New York, NY: Berghahn Books, 2008), 25.

4. René Lemarchand, "Introduction," in *Forgotten Genocides: Oblivion, Denial, and Memory*, ed. R. Lemarchand (Philadelphia, PA: University of Pennsylvania Press, 2011), 1–19.

5. In 2013, the Genocide Research Group was formed out of the concerted efforts to address just this paucity of research. The Genocide Research Group was formed by an interdisciplinary group of faculty affiliated with the Department of African and African American Studies, at Northeastern Illinois University in Chicago, and began as an effort to collaborate on ways to develop future projects that focused on genocide specifically within the contexts of Africa and the African diaspora. The members of the group quickly noticed parallels between their work, and by 2014, the group organized its first symposium, *Silencing Genocide in Africa and the African Diaspora*.

6. The exception to this is the recently published, *Genocide Studies and Prevention: Rethinking Genocide, Mass Atrocities, and Political Violence in Africa: New Directions, New Inquiries, and Global Perspectives*, 13, (2), 2019. In the editor's introduction, they clarify their focus as "an attempt to critically investigate the meaning of the conceptual labels used to make meaning of conflicts across Africa." (p. 8). The focus is on the use of terms like "genocide," "civil war," "religious violence,"

"ethnic violence," and "terrorism." The focus is on how these terms frame analytical structures through which violence is viewed, and not on the way genocide appears within these contexts. This exception, while extremely important, only proves the rule rather than works as counterfactual.

7. See Orlando Patterson, *Slavery and Social Death* (Cambridge, MA: Harvard University Press, 1984); Claudia Card, *Confronting Evil: Terrorism, Torture, Genocide* (Cambridge: Cambridge University Press, 2010); and more recently, see Alexander Weheliye, *Habeus Viscus: Racializing Assemblages, Biopolitics, and Black Feminist Theories of the Human* (Durham, NC: Duke University Press, 2014).

8. United Nation's *Convention on the Prevention and Punishment of the Crime of Genocide*, 1948.

9. See Anson Rabinbach, "The Challenge of the Unprecedented—Raphaël Lemkin and the Concept of Genocide," in *Simon Dubnow Institute Yearbook*, IV (Göttingen: Vandenhoeck & Ruprecht, 2005), 412–15; Tanya Elder, "What you See Before your Eyes: Documenting Raphaël Lemkin's Life by Exploring his Archival Papers, 1900–1959," *Journal of Genocide Research*, 7, (4), 2005, 486–99; Anton Weiss-Wendt, "Hostage of politics: Raphaël Lemkin on 'Soviet Genocide,'" *Journal of Genocide Research*, 7, (4), 2005, 551–59; Dominik Schaller and Jürgen Zimmerer, *The Origins of Genocide: Raphaël Lemkin as Historian of Mass Violence* (New York, NY: Routledge, 2013); *Journal of Genocide Research: New Approaches to Raphael Lemkin*, 15, (3), 2013; Douglas Irvin-Erickson, *Raphaël Lemkin and the Concept of Genocide* (Philadelphia, PA: University of Pennsylvania Press, 2016); *Genocide Studies and Prevention: Revisiting the Life and Work of Raphael Lemkin*, 13, (1), 2019.

10. Raphaël Lemkin's, *Axis Rule in Occupied Europe: Laws of Occupation, Analysis of Government, Proposal for Redress* (New York, NY: Columbia University Press, 1944).

11. Raphaël Lemkin, "The Germans In Africa," in *Lemkin on Genocide*, ed. S. Jacobs (Lanham, MD: Lexington Books, 2012), 189–222.

12. William Paterson and the Civil Rights Council, *We Charge Genocide: The Historic Petition to the United Nations for Relief from a Crime of the United States Government against the Negro People*, ed. William Patterson and Civil Rights Congress (New York, NY: International Publishers, 1951), 4.

13. Ibid., 196.

14. Steven Leonard Jacobs, "We Charge Genocide: A Historical Petition All but Forgotten and Unknown," in *Understanding Atrocities: Remembering, Representing, and Teaching Genocide*, ed. S. Murray (Alberta: University of Calgary Press, 2017), 125–43.

15. Raphaël Lemkin, "Nature of Genocide: Confusion with Discrimination Against Individuals Seen," *The New York Times, Letters to the Times*, Sunday, June 13, 1953.

16. The argument that Holocaust has been used as an example to deflect comparison with American slavery is well documented and is part of the argument of Lissa Skitolsky's contribution to this volume. More generally, traces of this argument can be seen as one of the motivating factors for a move toward a critical genocide studies

that is separate in identity from holocaust studies. In "Does the Holocaust Reveal or Conceal Other Genocides? The Canadian Museum of Human Rights and Grievable Suffering," A. Dirk Moses, makes just this argument. The essay appears in *Hidden Genocides: Power, Knowledge, Memory*, ed. A. Hinton, T. La Pointe, and D. Irvin-Erickson (New Brunswick, NJ: Rutgers University Press, 2014), 21–51. Beyond the critical argument, though, here is an emerging literature on this point of comparison that might be fruitfully engaged if the Holocaust was not seen as synonymous with the word "genocide." See, for example, Jonathan Wiesen's, "American Lynching and the Nazi Imagination: Race and Extra-Legal Violence in 1930s Germany," *German History*, 36, 1, 2018, 38–59.

17. *Colonialism and Genocide*, ed. A. Dirk Moses and Dan Stone (New York, NY: Routledge, 2006).

18. For this reason, the heavy focus on defining genocide, while important, has also worked to obscure both action and analysis. See A. Dirk Moses, "Conceptual Blockages and Definitional Dilemmas in the 'Racial Century': Genocides of Indigenous People and the Holocaust," *Patterns of Prejudice*, 36, (4), 2002, 7–36; David Moshman, "Conceptions of Genocide," in *The Historiography of Genocide*, ed. D. Stone (New York, NY: Palgrave Macmillan, 2010), 71—92; Kurt Mills, *International Responses to Mass Atrocities in Africa: Responsibility to Protect, Prosecute, and Palliate* (Philadelphia, PA: University of Pennsylvania Press, 2015).

19. See Levene, *Genocide in the Age of the Nation State, Vol. 1* and *Genocide in the Age of the Nation State, Vol. 2: The Rise of the West and the Coming of Genocide* (New York, NY: I.B. Tauris, 2013).

20. See Rob Nixon, *Slow Violence and the Environmentalism of the Poor* (Cambridge, MA: Harvard University Press, 2011).

Chapter 1

Burundi 1972

Remembering a Forgotten Genocide

René Lemarchand

No other state in Africa has experienced as many genocidal convulsions as has Burundi since its independence. Nor is any other state, at the time of this writing (2016), more vulnerable to a resumption of ethnic violence on a massive scale.

Behind the complicated chain of events that turned its two principal communities, Hutu and Tutsi, into "complementary enemies,"[1] one particularly gruesome episode stands out—the 1972 carnage, often referred to in Kirundi as *ikiza*, the scourge. Its lasting impact on Burundi's history recently came into focus when scores of Hutu politicians, most of them closely associated with President Nkuruzinza's embattled regime, many well known as "orphans of genocide," paid public but selective homage to the victims of the 1972 tragedy. Yet, to this day, it remains one of the most under-reported and least understood of the many bloodbaths of the last century.

The basic facts are reasonably well-established: a decade after its independence from Belgium in 1962, Burundi became the scene of massive violence when, in response to a localized Hutu-led insurrection, causing thousands of deaths among the Tutsi, anywhere from 150,000 to 200,000 Hutu civilians were massacred at the hands of a Tutsi-dominated army. I am old enough to remember the Burundi tragedy as if it happened yesterday; it is associated in my mind with the loss of many close friends. But what I find most striking in retrospect is the silence of the media surrounding the killings, in obvious contrast with the orgy of press coverage about the Rwanda bloodbath.

The Burundi genocide is not the only horror story that has fallen into oblivion. In a collaborative effort on the theme of forgotten genocides,[2] I have tried to give the place they deserve to such rarely remembered cases as the Herero of German Southwest Africa, the Kurds of Iraq, the Aborigines of Tasmania, the Assyrians in nineteenth-century Ottoman Turkey, the Hutu refugees from

Rwanda in eastern Congo, the Gypsies during Nazi rule, and the Tibetans in contemporary China. This is only a small sample. All are alike in the scale of the atrocities committed by one community against another, yet they seldom fit the same template. No less than the motives for murder, the underlying circumstances cover a wide spectrum, as do the lessons to be learned.

WHY REMEMBER?

Why bother to drag out of the shadows such appalling events, unfolding in faraway lands, decades if not centuries ago? The short answer is that they involve the lives and deaths of millions of people, who, for a variety of reasons, were wiped off the face of the earth. This is not a trivial matter. There is more to historical narratives than redeeming the memory of past atrocities. They help us think critically about the roots of human tragedies and their consequences. George Santayana's well-known aphorism—"those who cannot remember the past are condemned to repeat it"—is not the only reason why it behooves us as citizens, students, and academics, to shine a light on these abominations.[3] Burundi is one of several other examples in which a more clear-eyed and determined stand by US policy makers would have saved thousands of lives. As Samantha Power has convincingly argued in her outstanding, prize-winning investigation of the roots of genocide in Rwanda, Kosovo, Bosnia, and Cambodia,[4] the reason for our inaction is not to be found in our lack of resources, but our lack of will, an attitude only thinly disguised by pious references to *acts of genocide*, as distinct from genocide, or out of *respect for national sovereignty*. As we now realize, concern over being dragged into a very messy situation in a state about which we knew next to nothing, and where we had no obvious interest at stake, was the main reason for Clinton's decision not to intervene in Rwanda. The same is true of Burundi: it simply did not register on our radar as a place where our national interests were at stake.

There are important lessons to be learned from a sustained examination of such seldom-remembered atrocities.

- Contrary to what is sometimes taken for granted, genocides are not necessarily state-sponsored; they can also happen as bottom-up phenomena, rooted in grassroots enmities.
- The roles of victims and perpetrators are often blurred; a group that qualifies as a victimized community at one point in time can eventually emerge as a perpetrator at a later date, or vice versa.
- Although the concept of genocide suggests a deliberate intent to destroy human lives, the decision to exterminate entire communities can be

compressed into a very short period of time, sometimes a matter of hours or days.⁵
- Opinions to the contrary notwithstanding, social structure can act as a major propellant of violence. Where groups are vertically structured, with an ethnic minority at the top and the majority reduced to an inferior status, conflict can easily mutate into genocide.
- Genocide cannot be isolated from its wider geopolitical context, be it regional or global (as was the case during the Cold War). Here, again, Burundi offers a striking illustration of how the regional context helps explain the dynamics of insurgency, and the global context the reluctance of the United States to intervene.

On most of these points, the case of Burundi offers considerable supporting evidence.

RWANDA AND BURUNDI: DIVERGENT PATHS TO SELF-RULE

The histories of Rwanda and Burundi are closely interlinked. Neither is immune from the other's dysfunction. Often referred to as "false twins," the phrase hints at their common features. Before they became German colonies—and later League of Nations Mandates and, after World War II, UN trust territories under Belgian administration—they were small, ancient kingdoms, characterized by a highly stratified pecking order; both shared roughly the same ethnic map, with their respective rulers (*bami*, singular *mwami*) standing at the top of an elaborate hierarchy of chiefs and sub-chiefs. Where Burundi stood conspicuously apart from its neighbor to the north was in the far greater complexity and flexibility of its social structure and political institutions.⁶ In sharp contrast with Rwanda, where the Hutu-Tutsi conflict emerged as a critical issue as early as 1956 on the eve of independence and for some time thereafter, Burundi showed few signs of ethnic tension. The principal line of cleavage was not between Hutu and Tutsi but between princely factions, or *ganwa*. Rwanda is where Belgian rule faced its greatest challenge. Faced with mounting ethnic violence, and under considerable pressure from the UN Trusteeship Council to speed up the transition to independence, the Belgian authorities felt they had no other choice but to throw the full weight of their administrative and military power behind the nascent Hutu elites. Thus, while Rwanda acceded to independence as a republic under Hutu rule, Burundi remained a constitutional monarchy under a mixed Hutu/Tutsi government until its overthrow by the army in 1956.

The full story of Belgian involvement on the side of what came to be known as the Hutu "social revolution," from November 1959 to July 1962, has yet to be fully pieced together. What is beyond doubt is that the violence that broke out in 1959 is better seen as a Hutu-sponsored peasant revolt than a full-fledged revolution. What eventually transformed a peasant revolt into a political revolution was the decision of the Belgian Resident-General, Jean-Paul Harroy, to give virtually unlimited power to a military *résident spécial* (Colonel Logiest) to insure a Hutu victory at the polls. Besides providing extensive political and logistical support to the Hutu-dominated *Parti de l'Emancipation du Peuple Hutu* (Party for Hulu Emancipation, known by the abbreviation *Parmehutu*) Belgian administrators could count on the presence of scores of metropolitan paratroopers to maintain "peace and order," which in numerous instances meant a violent repression of the activities of Tutsi nationalists identified with the *Union Nationale Rwandaise* (Rwandese National Union, known by the abbreviation *Unar*). Tutsi civilians paid a heavy price: forced out of their homeland at gunpoint, tens of thousands found refuge in neighboring states.

As many as 40,000 Tutsi refugees fled to Burundi in the early 1960s; the significance of their role as a vector of conflict cannot be overrated. Besides alerting their Burundi kinsmen to the clear and present danger of a possible Hutu insurrection of the Rwandans, they stood as an auxiliary force should their assistance be needed. The influx of refugees is only one of the many factors behind the rising ethnic temperature in the years following independence; yet, there can be little question that its impact has been profound.

ANATOMY OF A BLOODBATH

The spark that ignited the 1972 genocide was the Hutu insurgency that broke out in late April 1972 in and around the lakeside communities of Rumonge and Nyanza Lac.[7] This can best be described as a local revolt instigated by the revolutionary incitements of a handful of Hutu opponents, some operating from Tanzania, others from the Zaire (formerly, the Congo). Little is known about their identity and ultimate political agenda, except that most of them were former students at the University of Bujumbura and shared a deep resentment of Tutsi rule. They found themselves socially marginalized and politically excluded as a result of the aborted coup in 1965, which was instigated by Hutu gendarmerie officers against the royal palace. They could hardly forget or forgive the heavy toll in human losses recently suffered by Hutu politicians, administrators, and soldiers at the hands of the Tutsi-dominated army, which included thousands of Hutus in the region of Muramvya in the north. Nor could they forget those arrested and summarily executed in

Bujumbura in 1969 under suspicion of plotting against the regime.[8] Although the government was largely in the hands of a Tutsi subgroup from the Bururi province in the south, and despite the growing intra-Tutsi tensions among the ruling elites, the insurgents drew no distinction between one group or the other.[9] Hundreds or possibly thousands of innocent Tutsi civilians were killed. The Tutsi-dominated army promptly quelled the uprising, and a modicum of peace was restored to the area in a matter of days.

No sooner had the suspected insurgents been eliminated than a more sustained, indiscriminate, and wide-ranging repression was set in motion that immediately took on the quality of a selective genocide.[10] It involved the systematic rounding up of every educated Hutu male, including school children, university students, civil servants, and NGO workers, across the country. Assisted by a fearsome youth militia—the *Jeunesses Révolutionnaires Rwagasore* (JRR)—and party activists identified with the predominantly Tutsi *Union pour le progrès national* (Union for National Progress, known by the abbreviation *UPRONA*), day after day army and police units arrested every Hutu in sight suspected of even a smattering of education. The manhunt went on for months. All were systematically killed, their bodies thrown into mass graves. Michael Hoyt, who served as US Deputy Chief of Mission in Bujumbura, described in his cables the sense of pervasive fear that seized the country:

> no respite, no letup. What is apparently a genocide continues. Arrests going on around the clock . . . Tutsi reprisals unabated . . . In the north the Hutu take cover upon arrival of any vehicle . . . In two days following July 14th, three new ditches filled with Hutu bodies near Bujumbura airport. Arrests have continued throughout the week in Bujumbura, in the hills around town, in Ngozi region and in central Burundi.

He goes on to add, "repression against Hutu is not simply one of killing, it is also an attempt to remove them from access to employment, property, education and the general chance to improve themselves."[11] Boniface Kiraranganiya, an eyewitness of princely origins *(ganwa)*, estimated the number of Hutu killed at 300,000. "If one day I lose my mind," he wrote, "the events of 1972 will have contributed to it by 95%." He described what he saw as "the paroxysm of madness, a perfect example of what man is capable of doing when all restraints are lifted, when there is nothing left to prevent him from giving free rein to his destructive instincts."[12] One of the first and most distinguished victims of the carnage was none other than deposed King Ntare, son of mwami Mwambutsa, who had just returned from Uganda after receiving assurances that his life would not be at risk. Ntare's fate was sealed by the fear he might have served as a rallying point for a Hutu insurrection.

The most amazing thing about this orgy of violence is how little impact it has had outside Burundi. Equally astonishing is that the only condemnation issued by the US government (though never made public) came from, of all people, Richard Nixon, in the form of handwritten remarks on a memo from Henry Kissinger. In the memo, he advised against US intervention, on the grounds that the killings posed no major threat to US interests. Nixon's statement captures his sense of anger in the face of what he referred to as a callous attitude and use of double standards:

> This is one of the most cynical, callous reactions of a great government to a terrible human tragedy I have seen. When the Paks try to put down a rebellion in East Pakistan, the world screams. When Indians kill a few thousand Paks, no one cares. Biafra stirs us because of Catholics, the Israeli Olympians [sic] because of Jews; the North Vietnamese bombings because of Communist leanings in our own establishment. But when 100,000, one third of the people of a black country [sic], are murdered, we say nothing because we must not make blacks look bad (except of course when Catholic blacks are killed). I do not buy this double standard. Tell the weak sisters in the Africa Bureau of State to give a recommendation as to how we can at least show moral outrage. And let's begin by calling our Ambassador immediately for consultation. Under no circumstances will I appoint a new Ambassador to present credentials to these butchers.[13]

Nixon's outburst provides a jarring note to the seeming indifference of the US public and policy makers at the time. Significantly, his sense of outrage did not resonate beyond the Oval Office. The assumption that came to dominate the State Department was that, however regrettable, the slaughter posed no direct or indirect threat to the US national interest.

Other factors intervened to keep the carnage out of the limelight. One is that human rights issues had yet to emerge as a significant source of public concern. Another has to do with the abysmal ignorance—among the attentive public and policy makers alike—surrounding Burundi's past and recent history. Yet another is the fact that, unlike what happened in Rwanda, the *génocidaires* won the day and took the opportunity to rewrite history from their own biased perspective, in effect claiming that the Hutu insurgency was the harbinger of a genocide of Tutsi—presumably, extraordinary dangers thus required extraordinary remedies.[14]

THE REGIONAL FALLOUT

The 1972 bloodletting carried far-reaching consequences within and outside Burundi's boundaries. For the next twenty years, Burundi was a state entirely controlled by elements of the Tutsi minority. The virtual absence of qualified Hutu candidates to hold responsible positions in the government and the administration made Tutsi hegemony a *normal* state of affairs, and a guarantee of peace for the foreseeable future.

The huge exodus of refugees radically transformed the social landscape of the host countries while sowing the seeds of countless conflicts over land inside Burundi. As tens of thousands of Hutu families were forced out of their homelands, their houses and landed property ended up, for the most part, in the hands of Tutsi claimants. Restoring their lost properties to the original owners is a hugely complicated problem. Of all the issues inherited from the 1972 crisis, it remains one of the most potentially explosive.

Not until 1993 would the Hutu be given another chance to gain control of their destinies: in the wake of another Hutu-Tutsi confrontation and under considerable external pressure, notably from the United States, the Tutsi strongman, Pierre Buyoya, agreed to hold free and fair multiparty elections. Although Hutu candidates scored a landslide victory, the verdict of the polls was quickly reversed when the army seized power, killing the first popularly elected Hutu president, Melchior Ndadaye, along with four of his closest political friends. In retrospect, the assassination of Ndadaye must be seen as the game-changing event from which Burundi never fully recovered, and the shock waves of which had a significant impact on the sequence of events leading to the Rwanda genocide. Besides unleashing a vicious, ten-year civil war that took an estimated 100,000 lives, it drove a deep wedge between moderates and extremists among Hutu activists and presumptive power-holders and gave a decisive moral boost to the organizers of mass murder in Rwanda. It is sadly ironic—as well as a commentary on the cruel tit-for-tat reciprocity of ethnic violence across boundaries—that many of the Hutu elements who found asylum in Rwanda during and after the 1972 crisis quickly retooled themselves into murderers of Tutsi civilians during the Rwanda genocide.

THE CONTINUING RELEVANCE OF 1972

As Burundi lurches toward semi-anarchy in the wake of President Nkurunziza's decision to run for an unprecedented third term,[15] in what ways can the events of 1972 help us understand the continuing violence?

Although the triggering factor behind the crisis bears no direct relationship to the 1972 bloodbath, the connecting links between the two are difficult to ignore. Again, even though the conflict is political in nature, involving Hutu and Tutsi on both sides of the fence on the issue of Nkurunziza's blatant violation of the constitution, the possibility of the simmering conflict morphing into a genocide cannot be dismissed.

Few reminders of Burundi's blood-stained trajectory are more poignant than the number of Hutu supporters of Nkurunziza who would not hesitate to describe themselves as *"les orphelins du genocide,"* or the orphans of genocide, echoing Alain Nyamitwe's posthumous homage to the five immediate members of his family—his father and four uncles.[16] Today, there are thousands of politically conscious Hutu who were toddlers or infants in 1972, and who grew up with continual reminders of why they became orphans. They appear determined to prevent history from repeating itself, even if it means propping up a regime fatally discredited by its appalling human rights abuses. Exactly how this common awareness of their tragic past may affect the destinies of their country is impossible to predict. Public acknowledgement of the crimes committed by the 1972 *génocidaires* will not bring impunity to an end; at worst, it could even stimulate revanchist sentiment and help justify gross human rights violations.

What gives credibility to this nightmare scenario is the repetitiveness of ethnic confrontations. One of the most consequential and least remembered took place in 1995 and resulted in the deliberate killing of scores of Hutu students at the hand of Tutsi-led militias and police units.[17] Now serving as Nkurunziza's minister of foreign affairs, Alain Nyamitwe's brush with death on that occasion is recounted in considerable detail in his autobiographical narrative.[18] Inscribed on the roster of victims supplied by the author (including their names, disciplines, and institutional affiliations) is the sheer depth of hatred evinced by Tutsi militias, most notably the *Sans échec et sans défaite*—led by a defrocked Dominican priest—as they went about the grim task of cleansing the Bujumbura campus of Hutu students. As happened in 1972 and 1993 after Ndadaye's assassination, generations of future Hutu elites were simply wiped out.

Perhaps the most intriguing of the legacies inherited from the country's genocidal past lies in the bizarre born-again religiosity displayed by Nkurunziza and his wife. Just as a great many Hutu in 1972 were devotees of the Pentecostal Church,[19] the presidential couple takes great pride in proclaiming themselves Christian. Nkurunziza himself went so far as to boast that he was elected to execute God's mission and that he knew about his victory from prophecies long before his election in 2005.[20] Regardless of how far Pentecostal beliefs can help elucidate his decision to run for a third term, his religious pretensions are difficult to reconcile with his regime's appalling human rights record.[21]

Setting the historical record straight is essential for any society trying to come to terms with its genocidal past. Not everyone would agree, however, about the merits of remembering past atrocities. In a brilliant and controversial essay, David Rieff makes a case for collective amnesia as a preferred strategy for countering the danger of revanchist claims: for the sake of reconciliation and compromise, his general argument holds that it is essential to know how to forgive and forget.²² Perhaps a more persuasive argument might be to establish when to remember and when to forget. On the strength of the evidence from Burundi, the case for remembering seems difficult to repudiate. To do so would insure the continuation of impunity, the root cause of the crimes committed by both sides. Only by resurrecting past ignominies can one establish the responsibilities of Hutu and Tutsi in driving their country to the edge of the abyss. Only by remembering the horrific killings committed in 1972 and beyond can proper homage be paid to their countless victims.

NOTES

1. The phrase is borrowed from Germaine Tillon's work on the war for Algerian independence, *Les ennemis complémentaires* (Paris: Editions de Minuit, 1960).

2. *Forgotten Genocides: Oblivion, Denial and Memory*, ed. René Lemarchand (Philadelphia, PA: University of Pennsylvania Press, 2011).

3. George Santayana, *Life of Reason: Reason in Common Sense* (Amherst, NY: Prometheus Books, 1998), 394.

4. Samantha Power, *A Problem from Hell: America and the Age of Genocide* (New York, NY: Basic Books, 2002).

5. For a telling example see André Guichaoua's ground-breaking discussion of the Rwanda genocide in his *From War to Genocide: Criminal Politics in Rwanda, 1990–1994* (Madison, WI: University of Wisconsin Press, 2015).

6. For an interesting short analysis of their conflicted trajectories, see Samuel Huntington, *Political Order in Changing Societies* (New Haven, NJ: Yale University Press, 1968), 171–73.

7. For a fuller discussion, see René Lemarchand, "The Burundi Killings of 1972," *Online Encyclopedia of Mass Violence*, 2008, http://www.massviolence.org/The-Burundi-Killings-of-1972.

8. See René Lemarchand, *Rwanda and Burundi* (New York, NY: Praeger Publishers, 1970), 416–35.

9. In the course of an interview with this writer one reliable missionary source, Msgr. Bududira, a Tutsi, estimated the number of Tutsi civilians killed at 5,000.

10. See René Lemarchand, *Selective Genocide in Burundi* (London: Minority Rights Group, 1973). The phrase "selective genocide" has a curious pedigree. It was first used in 1971 by Archer Blood, the US Consul General in Dhaka during the violent break away of East Pakistan, now Bangladesh, to characterize the murderous repression of the US-backed Pakistani army Also see Gary J. Bass, *The Blood Telegram: Nixon, Kissinger and a Forgotten Genocide* (New York, NY: Vintage Books, 2014). It was later picked up by Michael Hoyt, Deputy Chief of Mission (DCM) in Bujumbura in one of his cables to the State Department, until resurrected as the title of my 1973 report to the Minority Rights Group.

11. The quotes are from the cables sent out from the Burundi embassy by Michael Hoyt, DCM, here cited from my book, *The Dynamics of Violence in Central Africa* (Philadelphia, PA: University of Pennsylvania Press, 2009), 136 and 137.

12. Boniface Kirranganiya, *Vérité sur le Burundi* (Sherbrooke: Editions Naaman, 1985), 76.

13. I am grateful to Christian Desroches, a former graduate student of mine at Concordia University for sharing this extraordinary document, reproduced from my *Forgotten Genocides*, 38.

14. In their coauthored work, *Burundi 1972: Au bord des genocides* (Paris: Karthala, 2007), Jean-Pierre Chrétien and Jean-Francois Dupaquier make the same unwarranted assumption: given the genocidal intentions of the Hutu insurgents the brutality of the Tutsi repression is easy to understand, if not condone.

15. See "Burundi: Anatomie du troisième mandate," *Crisis Group*, 235, May 20, 2016.

16. Alain Aimé Nyamitwe, *J'ai échappé au massacre de l'université du Burundi, 11 juin 1995* (Paris: L'Harmattan, 2006).

17. For a devastating and entirely credible account of the atrocities committed at the time through many parts of Burundi by the Tutsi-dominated armed forces, see the illuminating narrative authored by a former US ambassador to Burundi and his wife, Robert Krueger and Kathleen Tobin Krueger, *From Bloodshed to Hope in Burundi: Our Embassy Years During Genocide* (Austin, TX: University of Texas Press, 2008). Strongly criticized by what some State Department officials saw as an unwarranted pro-Hutu attitude Ambassador Krueger was soon replaced by a more pliant candidate. No one did more to bring his career to a halt than Howard Wolpe, later to serve as the US Special Envoy to Burundi. "State," wrote Wolpe, "was hugely embarrassed by Krueger's conduct, and felt that they had to remove him from the scene. He became identified with a pro-Hutu perspective and so demonized by all Tutsi that he became dysfunctional as a diplomat. He was removed before I began my role as Special Envoy." Howard Wolpe to this writer, February 26, 2008.

18. Nyamitwe, *J'ai échappé au massacre de l'université*.

19. I am grateful to Gunilla Nyberg Oaskarsson, a Swedish historian, for sharing with me her expertise on the history of the Pentecostal Church, which she describes as "the biggest Protestant Church in Burundi;" her doctoral dissertation, *Le movement pentecostiste – une communauté alternative au sud du Burundi (1935–1960)* has yet to be translated into English.

20. In her memoir, the First Lady of Burundi explains how her husband decided to run for reelection in 2010: "Towards the end of 2009 we gathered to commune with God from deep within ourselves: 'if this is not your will, Lord, we do not wish to relive the experience of the last five years' . . . If it went against God's will, he would not put his name forward . . . . I asked him if he was going to go for election. 'Yes because God has accepted it.' And he ran for the next mandate." Whether God accepted his decision to run for a third mandate remains unclear. Denise Bucumi-Nkurunziza, *The Power of Hope* (Paris: L'Harmattan, 2013), 147.

21. There have been no fewer than 651 cases of torture were reported between April 2015 and April 2016. Most of the tortures have been committed by the

intelligence service (*Service national de renseignement*), the police, and the ruling party's youth league (*imbonerakure*). See Human Rights Watch (URW), *Burundi: Intelligence Services Torture Suspected Opponents*, July 7, 2016, https://www.hrw.org/news/2016/07/07/burundi.

22. David Rieff, *Against Remembrance* (Melbourne: Melbourne University Press, 2011). Also see his exchange with Joshua Oppenheimer, "How Different are Victims from Victimizers?" *Foreign Policy*, September–October 2015, 31.

Chapter 2

Repenser pour mieux panser (Remembering for Better Healing)

A Survivor's Account of the 1972 Burundi Genocide

Jeanine Ntihirageza

Had the world said *never again* in 1972 regarding genocide in Burundi, perhaps it would have been prevented in Rwanda, its next-door neighbor. Unfortunately, the world chose to be quiet then. Between May and August 1972, a carefully planned massacre of Hutu elites—businessmen, teachers, students, army officers, and members of the clergy—was methodically carried out. Although the number of victims will never be known, estimates range between 150,000 and 300,000.[1] Heavy silence settled on the survivors, imposed by the Tutsi-dominated government. In this narrative, for the first time publicly, I discuss what it was like to be deprived of mourning for loved ones, to be accused of being a traitor while being terrorized. It is my hope that this account will contribute, albeit in a small way, to healing deep emotional wounds from genocide.

René Lemarchand, in his article "Le génocide de 1972 au Burundi: Les Silences de l'Histoire" (The Silence of History) points out that the intention of his paper is not to revive hatred or refresh wounds of history but to revisit them in order to better heal them.[2] Recalling the parallel horrors that hit the Hutu in Burundi and the Tutsi in Rwanda, the duty to remember emerges as a key imperative along with the necessity to fill the breach that separates the past and the future. Painful as it is to evoke the past, it has to be reckoned with. Silence is the first step toward reconstructing history and is also the source of hatred, which nourishes the complicity of oblivion and the powers that be.[3] "*Repenser pour mieux panser les blessures de l'histoire* [Remembering to better bandage the wounds of history]," writes Lemarchand. We should all try it if we have been silenced for any reason! After all, many fields of study and practice, particularly in the treatment of trauma, are based on this reality. I owe the beginning of the healing process to Lemarchand's article because it helped me understand what was wrong with me. I had never mourned my father, half-brother and cousins. Their loss was all bottled up inside me.

ETHNOGRAPHIC SETTING

In 1972, Burundi's population was composed of three different ethnic groups. Of these, 85 percent was Hutu—the majority in number, but a minority in power. The Tutsi, minority in number but majority in power, constituted 14 percent, whereas the Twa were only 1 percent of the population and were the forgotten ones in power aspirations. Through the years, colonizers, anthropologists, and historians have tried to come up with a composite of physical traits that distinguish these groups to no avail. They themselves have made fatal mistakes by killing members of their own groups because they relied on those misleading physical features established by Europeans. In fact, even these population ratios are misleading.[4] Research has repeatedly shown that there is no truth-value in these separate identities because they are not natural, no less superficial than the boundaries between African countries. According to Ibrahim Omer, "In the early 1930s, for example, the Belgians in Burundi classified an owner with ten or more cows as Tutsi and a poor citizen as Hutu regardless of ethnic identity."[5] A common practice, during colonization, in Burundi and Rwanda, was the process of "kwihutura," that is, to shed hutuness by becoming Tutsi. The candidate had to pay a number of cows and pots of beer to the king. Tutsification was only accessible to those who were wealthy and who had understood that being Tutsi came with perks such as social and political power. Despite the elitism of Tutsi versus the Hutu, the two groups did not kill each other. According to Omer,[6] "Even in the colonial era—when Belgium ruled the area, after taking it from Germany in 1916—the two groups lived as one, speaking the same language, intermarrying, and obeying a nearly godlike Tutsi king."[7] The independence of Burundi was a turning point.

Tutsi, while minority in number, were majority in power for decades in Burundi. They occupied key posts in the army, the justice system, education and many other institutions locally and nationally. They could make unjust decisions and get away with it. During and after the 1972 Hutu massacre by Tutsi army and militia, the Tutsi government was able to trick the entire world by convincing everyone that nothing had happened. To this day, the 1972 Burundi genocide is quite unknown outside academia, particularly in the West.

Never Mourned Individually or Collectively as a Nation

In addition to the efforts of concealing the crime from the international community, the Tutsi government managed to convince genocide survivors that those who died deserved to die though there was no clear explanation why they deserved to die. Terror spread so fast that no one, among survivors, could ask questions. Because people were taken away and never came back or simply just vanished, nobody seemed, on the surface, to be directly responsible for their disappearance. It was then decreed that there would be no mourning locally or nationally. Anybody who was caught mourning a loved one during the scourge *ikiza*, which became the name of the 1972 genocide, had to undergo some form of punishment.

Those in power at that time told the country to refer to the killings as an *event*. It was quite convenient for the government to use the word *ikiza*, sometimes translated as *event* for such a horrific act instead of massacre or, better yet, genocide, so that the national consciousness does not memorize any responsibility, no more than natural disasters such as hurricanes and storms can be blamed on any one. Survivors did exactly as they were told: you didn't see anything, you don't blame anybody, and you don't mourn!

I thought I had become the master of *concealment and denial* until forty years later, when unwelcome memories began to invade my work and life. The first time buried memories bubbled up is when I was asked to translate for a caseworker and a Burundian refugee woman who had resettled in Chicago from a Tanzania refugee camp. As this woman recounted what had happened to her, I lost control of my own emotions that I didn't even know were buried inside. Somehow I almost wanted to ask her, *"Have you seen my father?"* I cried uncontrollably to the point that the caseworker told me to go take care of myself. My consciousness was altered again when I visited the *Forbidden Art* exhibit—Auschwitz Death Camp Art at Northeastern Illinois University on display on October 20, 2012. Oh, how tough that was! By the third image, caught by surprise, I experienced uncontrollable sorrow and wept, just remembering that the vast majority of the Hutu killed in 1972 didn't leave much in terms of visuals. Most recently, when I attempted to collaborate with a colleague on a language of violence project, I could not even start to brainstorm ideas. Each time I tried to remember the words that were used to describe us, Hutu, I broke down and became emotionally paralyzed.

The most telling source of emotional outpouring happened when I watched *Hotel Rwanda* with my husband. Almost every scene in the movie took me back to what could have happened to my people. Numerous questions invaded my mind. Did the trucks drive over my father's body the way it was depicted in the movie about genocide in Rwanda? Was he chopped up the way the genocidaires did it in the movie? The loss of my father, my half-brother, and my cousins to the 1972 genocide in Burundi felt as if it had just happened. I could not control the emotions that bubbled over. I thought I had forgiven *THEM*. *THEM*, those who killed my father; *THEM*, those who killed my dearest half-brother (growing up, until I lost him, I actually thought he was perfect!); *THEM*, those who killed my cousins; *THEM*, those who took my father's property (stores, boutiques, restaurant, merchandise, tools, etc.) so that I went from a comfortable life to quite poor in a very short period of time. Yes, it is still very painful to remember it all.

At some point, I thought I had forgiven them. But, no! A myriad of emotions and questions flooded my mind. How could our village neighbors, who we knew so well take away our loved ones? How could they commit such atrocious acts to innocent people with whom they had shared so much? How did our deaf and mute neighbor manage to trick tough, tall, and strong Hutu men into following him to watch the invisible enemy for the so-called national security? Somehow some representative Tutsi, all neighbors, convinced Hutu in my family and beyond that there was an enemy who was about to attack the nation and invited them to go somewhere on top of some hill to guard the village. Of course, they never came back! If I had forgiven THEM, then I surely was far from forgetting. The emotions were raw. I cried uncontrollably during the movie and afterward. For three days, I did not get out of bed. Then it all came back as if I were eleven years old all over again.

In each of these cases, I had to come to terms with the reality: that an unbearable deep-seated pain was still there and that I needed to deal with it. Usually, when I talked about Hutu-Tutsi relations in Burundi and the 1972 killings, I somehow managed to remove myself from that reality and that discourse.

What Do You Mean I'm Hutu?

I'm thirteen and it's 1974, my first semester at Rutovu boarding high school.[8] We have a whole hour of recess after lunch. Girls are playing dodgeball in the schoolyard. So much goes on there. Some seem to be absolutely cruel, targeting this one girl during the game. One of my friends who came from the same hometown and from the same elementary school, Neroze, a little older than me, approaches me and says, "Do you know why Naviya is throwing the ball at Derive with so much meanness?" I say, "no." She says, "It's because Derive is Hutu." I ask her what Naviya is, to which she responds, "Tutsi." I then ask what she herself is and what I am. This is the first time I hear the four-letter-word "H-U-T-U" applied to me. You see, the only Hutu I knew until then was the family who has to regularly and forever be bringing a portion of their crops to my family for having accepted *one* cow as a gift from my father.[9] A million and one questions and thoughts cascade rapidly through my mind. Why? When? Who? Was my father born Hutu? Did he choose it? Why didn't he choose to be Tutsi if being Hutu can kill him? Why do all these girls seem to know this business of Hutu and Tutsi and I have no idea?

Neroze proceeds right there, on that schoolyard, to inform me that my father had been killed, in 1972, two years earlier, because he was Hutu. Wait a minute! Oh no, my father is not dead; he is in Tanzania and is coming back soon, so I was told by one of my older half-sisters. I later understood that they did it to protect me because they knew how extremely close I was to my father. I am staggered by the awareness that I may not see my father, my hero, again on this earth. The idea that he is gone pierces my heart. There are no right words to express the pain I'm experiencing at this moment.

Neroze is also quick to tell me that my mother is Tutsi. Tutsi? Why didn't she choose to be like my father and me? I have never heard of the word Tutsi, except when Tutsi women referred to each other as *Mututsikazi* [female Tutsi], a term of endearment. More questions and thoughts race through my head. I couldn't wait to go home during Christmas break to ask her. I am Hutu; she is Tutsi; my father was Hutu. That I am mixed doesn't count for anything, no more than a mixed black and white person cannot be white. In Burundi if your father is Tutsi, you're automatically Tutsi and if your father is Hutu, you're Hutu. Patrilineality par excellence for a concept that's almost arbitrary!

The schoolyard became a place where I learned about the peculiar world of identity and power, which I didn't understand experientially. This is where I lost the innocence of immediate identification toward others. The world of humans around me became instantly binary: Hutu and Tutsi. My understanding of my identity and the Hutu/Tutsi divide happened suddenly and turned my world upside down. It's almost as if I would have preferred to be ignorant about the whole thing.

Making Friends: A Careful Process/Gauging Identity

Derive approaches and hesitantly asks, "*Wewe urafise Papa?*" ("Do you have a father?" which implies "Is your father dead or alive?") A few minutes before, I would have said yes, perhaps with a clarification that he was a refugee in Tanzania. She then says, "When did he die?" I say, "1972," repeating what I have just heard from Neroze. Her face relaxes because she understands that there is a 99 percent chance that I am Hutu if my father died in 1972. Implications: he was killed and therefore he was Hutu. If my father was Hutu, then I am Hutu. There is then the possibility that we could potentially become friends since she herself is Hutu.

It turns out there were three Hutu girls and seven Hutu boys out of eighty students in the two seventh grade classes. Since the population ratio in

Burundi was and still is about 85percent Hutu, 14 percent Tutsi, and 1 percent Twa, how did it happen that these classes had the majority Tutsi students from a minority population? Certainly not because of the neighborhood or location, that is, not regional since Tutsi and Hutu live together, not religious since both ethnic groups practiced the same religion, primarily Christianity. There was no official criterion. The answer, though, does not require a lot of ingenuity.

All the Family Pictures Gone, Lost Memories!

When I got home from school for Christmas break, I found to my great dismay, that my mother had burned every single picture we had because my father was on each of them and my relatives convinced her not to keep a picture of a dead person. They explained to her that this would be *kumusimbura*, reminding the survivors of his death, which is a social taboo, particularly if he had been killed during the 1972 genocide. My father had taken pride in having every child's birth recorded with a picture until he died. I loved those pictures! Now they were gone! People were expected to act and go on with their lives as though everything was normal, nothing had changed, only everything had changed and we couldn't talk about it and could not share any memories. We had to pretend we forgave before we even remembered. Today, when other cultures memorialize genocide victims using pictures and other artifacts their loved ones left, my people will sadly not have much from before 1972 due to these cultural taboos.

My Father and Me!

I am the first-born of my parents' ten children (my older half-brothers and sisters lived on their own). Even if we lived on a farm, I certainly did not feel the pressures of being the oldest because we had many housekeepers and farm employees, some to take care of cooking and cleaning, some to look after cows, and some to take care of the fields. Somehow, I was spoiled. I got almost everything I wanted then. My wish list wasn't usually long: candy, sugar, bread, that's about it. My father always made me feel like I was the best thing that ever happened to this world and I was eager to please him. He took pride in my school success and I worked very hard to make sure I was among the top five students every year. He would take my report card and walk around with it among his business colleagues at the marketplace, talking about how smart I was. I beamed with joy. I may have been the first girl in our small town to ride on the back of her father's bike. Yes, I was very special to him! Though we had many people in our home, he always wanted me to serve him food when he ate. This was our routine: once ready to eat, he would call out my name (well, usually shortened): *Ntihirage*! Wherever I was, I would drop everything and rush to him, joyfully.[10] Then he would eat. It's strange, just remembering that call brings warmth to my heart and tears to my eyes as if it just happened.

We did not go through this routine on Saturday morning of April 29, 1972. You see, the family woke up early that morning because my father was planning a trip to buy merchandise for his stores, as he always did on alternating Saturdays or Wednesdays. This time was even more special because he was going to get his first new car for the occasion of his eldest son's wedding. The road had been paved all the way to our house, just for that occasion. This was rare in Burundi in 1972! That's how respected my father, Rwasa Bonaventure, was! By the time I woke up he was walking along the fence of our huge compound. I heard my mother remind him that he was going to be late. He usually met up with other merchants at the shopping center. One of them, Baragafise, a Tutsi, worked in one of our boutiques.

That morning, according to routine, one of the housekeepers put breakfast on the table. That was a sign that I needed to be close by in case my father called my name. I waited and waited . . . . He kept walking back and forth aimlessly along the fence. He looked very sad. At some point, I think he realized he was about to delay other people. He took his bag and left. He didn't eat breakfast that morning. He never called my name again! How much I miss him!

My oldest half-brother, Onesphore Nimbona (a businessman just like our father), was to get married on the following Saturday (yes, Saturday! Not everybody could afford Saturday weddings; most people got married on Wednesday because it was much cheaper or free.) My mother was drying grain on the ground in preparation for local beer for the wedding. I was helping her, well, in the most ineffective way (I kept scattering the grain).

Then almost from nowhere, we heard screaming. First it was just a few people, then more voices broke out, crying: "*Hunga, hunga abansi b'igihugu baduteye* [Run/flee, run/flee! Enemies of the country have attacked us]!" Within a very short time, a large group of us began walking toward the parish church, which seemed like the safest place to be. However, the church was too far—about 4 kilometers from our house—so the adults, including my mother, decided to gather at a neighbor's house instead. That way, they could watch out for the enemy together and be able to feed their children. I was one of those children, but I could not eat. I loved milk more than a cat; it was a fact known to all our neighbors. However, the milk would not settle in my stomach that day. I loved pumpkin (I used to bite them raw, a fact also known to the neighbors; older people used to remind me of that). That day I vomited the pumpkin, too, right after I ate it. When I was older and my mother and I talked about that day, she told me she knew right away that something had happened to my father just by seeing how sick I was.

Toward the evening, we were told to return home. During the following days, male Tutsi neighbors came to recruit my cousins, Ntigahera and Sababu, to serve as guards *at some unidentified location*, staying awake to make sure the enemy did not surprise the village. Only later would I discover that this had just been a lie to take these men away. They never came back. One of the hardest moments during this time was when my soon-to-be-married half-brother, Onesphore, was arrested. The local administration claimed that they needed to ensure that he wasn't involved in any "wrongdoing." My oldest half-sister Lehokadiya, knowing how close I was to Onesphore, took me to visit him in jail. He was locked in a tiny hut far from the administration building, closer to the bush. Lehokadiya tried to lift me so that I could see his face through a little round window that looked like a hole. It was very hard to see anything inside. I barely saw his eyes. I had nightmares about this moment for many years. In some dreams, the hut appeared like a huge round rock locked by a tiny door so that no human being could go in and out. I cried all the way home. He never came back. I never saw him again. Oh, how much it hurts! What do I remember about him? He was quiet, smart, tall, and handsome. People in the village and beyond loved him so much. He was going to marry a teacher, which was a big deal then for a businessman.

It is around this time that my half-sisters, Lehokadiya and Nasitaziya, told me that *ikiza* had taken many people, but that our father was able to flee to Tanzania. He would come back once the country had regained peace. How much I wish that had been true!

The Horror of Walking Home Alone

My elementary school was located 2.5 miles from my home. Before 1972, I would walk to my father's work place and then he would give me a ride home on his bike. I remember those bike rides with intense nostalgia. When he couldn't give a ride, I would walk home all alone peacefully without anything or anyone bothering me, though I was very young. After 1972, a group of girls and boys started mocking me. They would gather in one place, *mu Kiziba*, a large roundabout, and would wait for me there. They would torture me physically and with words. They would call me names, but at that time I had no idea what they were talking about. I remember them criticizing the size of my nose (later on I understood that a large nose was one of the Hutu features), talking about how I used up more oxygen than they did and that soon all the air would be gone because of me. I was terrified of this group. That's when I learned to run fast, which later served me well because I became a track and field athlete in high school.

A Tutsi Whose Tutsiness Did Not Protect Her Family

Did I mention that my mother is Tutsi? Before the *ikiza*, other Tutsi were happy enough that she had married a rich man. Afterward, they did not hesitate to torment her, uttering statements such as *warahemutse* and *waragotse*, both words referring to the despicable act of marrying a Hutu. I remember one day when one of my mother's friends, a Tutsi, called out to my mother, saying, "*Mututsika* [short for *Mututsikazi*]," my mother, upset, responded with a very strong, convincing, powerful voice, "*Ntuze usubire kunyita umututsikazi!* [Don't ever call me a Tutsi!]" I never asked her why, but one can only guess.

I still believe that Baragafise, my father's employee, must have known what happened to my father. Once he came back, by himself, from the trip, he decided to change the locks on all the stores, boutiques (including Onesphore's boutique), and restaurant. The buildings and the contents all automatically became his property, which he eventually shared with his sons. Other Tutsi who knew, somehow, that my father was not coming back came to our house to take a bicycle, a platform scale and weights, and many other items of value. I remember helplessly watching my mother trying, after they had come a couple of times, to fight for the little we had left. Of course, they overpowered her and took the last bit they could take. They also took possession of two very large plots of land that my father had purchased to make sure his family had enough farming space. On Tuesday, June 17, 2014, we finally regained possession of one of them.

From that moment on I grew up very poor. My mother worked very hard to make sure her children didn't grow up hungry, but at times we were. There were times when she didn't eat so that we could. This is still very painful to think about! Gradually, as I grew older and became increasingly aware of what had happened, I was disoriented by how the world around me had irreparably changed. My mother vowed to protect her dear Hutu children to the point of being treated as a social outcast by some members of her family.

Heavy Silence Fell on Us

"Zip it!" was what I thought I heard from the clouds, the banana trees, corn, sorghum, the bushes, mountains and valleys; "zip it!" from anywhere and anything. They seemed to all say in unison "Zip it!" You don't cry, you don't mourn because your father, your half-brother, your cousins and all those other men that were killed deserved to die, so we were told. Maybe my mother heard the same voices since she never said anything until I was much older. I remember her going to the bathroom to cry because she could not do it in public. I had no idea why she was crying. I would just look at her wondering why she was crying and hiding it. The government taught us not to mourn our dead, never to talk about it. It was as if it wasn't just the government and its representatives that would punish us if we did, but all the forces of nature that surrounded us. "They would certainly find out, they seem to be everywhere." That's the kind of fear that gripped me after losing some of the anchors in my life very dear to my heart. Widows and orphans didn't bury their loved ones and, to make matters worse, they were forbidden from mourning, at the risk of beating and/or imprisonment!

Blaming the Victim

We were told that those who were killed were the enemies of the nation. The survivors also became, by association, enemies of the nation for life and we were treated as such in the years that followed. We were called belittling names: *Igihere* "bedbug," *inyankaburundi/abansi b'igihugu*, "enemies of the nation," *abicanyi/genocidaires* "murderers," *inkozi z'ikibi* "evil doers," *abamenja/abayahudi/abayuda* (related Judas Iscariot) "traitors," and *mayimayi murere*, a nickname for rebels of that time. We began speaking in code for any message related to 1972 genocide. For example: "*Ça s'est passé en 27.* [It happened in 27.]" In this statement, "27" refers to 1972, in which 72 is reversed to 27. We were members of the majority ethnic group, as I came to understand later on, yet we felt like complete outcasts. Anything negative was portrayed as Hutu. On the other hand, the word "Tutsi" instantly implied all the best qualities, such as prestigious, beautiful, elegant, powerful, and valuable. Sadly, the linguistic division was binary; it evoked a bad or good, a Hutu or Tutsi, and that would continue for years to come.

It's Not My Fault That I'm Hutu!

The consequences of *ikiza* were appalling beyond the loss of lives. One of the most noticeable impacts of the *ikiza* on an eleven-year-old is the loss of one of her best friends. By fifth grade I had two best friends. We did everything together. We planned everything together. We shared everything. For example, they were the first ones to try on my new blue sandals. At that time, I may have been one of four or five children who owned a pair of shoes in the whole elementary school. School felt safe because I had these two friends. That did not last long. Without any apparent reason, one of them decided to not talk to us anymore, let alone hang out with us. Somehow she must have known more than we knew since she didn't want to talk to us again. When I approached her, she just moved away. Even when I brought our favorite drink, water plus sugar (this was a luxury since many households then could not afford sugar), she absolutely had nothing to do with us. It turns out she was Tutsi and we were Hutu. I still wonder how she discovered who was what since I didn't find out these differences until I was in the boarding school. She joined the group of girls we never wanted to connect with because they were not the nicest. We subsequently experienced loneliness, exclusion, teasing, etc. We had no idea why our friend left us and why many of the other girls referred to us as *abamenja* (traitors).

My awareness of my *Hutuness* clarified behaviors that I could not understand in the aftermath of the genocide. The most exciting summer activity used to be visiting my uncles, aunts and cousins on my mother's side. Unfortunately, after 1972, visiting some of these families became a burden. When my sister and I went to visit, we immediately felt we did not belong. I remember with chagrin watching my cousins and their friends giggle and whisper messages that we could not hear. They used to mock the size and shapes of our heads. We were not cool anymore. I came to understand that not only were we not rich anymore, we were also HUTU. As I grew older, I came to realize that they treated us that way because we were Hutu and they were Tutsi.

One of my paternal aunts is married to a Tutsi. I remember things slowly becoming weird. My cousins became colder and somehow they gained more self-esteem than before (they were from very poor families compared to us). They didn't want to play with us anymore. I could not just visit their house as I used to as they stopped coming to visit us. Something had gone wrong except that I had no idea what it was at that time. Everything seemed very strange. One of their sons, though, joined the military. Our relationships kept changing for the worse. Their family instantly gained high regard from the other members of my extended family. My aunt's husband, Myiruko, overnight, became *umukuru wa Gacimbiri* (chief of the local subdivision). No case of dispute was settled in his absence. Everyone had to wait for him. One day a group of the wise men of the village sat for a long time outside a compound. It was usually a signal that there had been some kind of discord. Tired of waiting, they sent me to fetch Myiruko so that they could start settling the case. Almost overnight, he gained power and people in the village constantly took pots of beer and other gifts to his family. He and his extended family were gradually treated as superior and we gradually felt quite inferior. At least among kids, that's how it felt. Grownups did not explain anything. Looking back, I can't help but wonder what triggered, and who dictated, the change locally. How much I wish I could talk to my aunt to know exactly what was going on inside her home.

*****

At a conference on Art and Violence at Northeastern Illinois University on October 14, 2016, I attended a workshop on using art for healing. The presenter asked the participants to use drawing and painting to express a violent experience. The moment that came back vividly to me was when my father was killed. I was in the middle of the common area of the neighbor's compound (my mother, my siblings, and I went to be with other villagers). I remember momentarily feeling completely alone on arid ground and there seemed to be an abyss between the living and me and I was engulfed in this wide lifeless circle. This time was followed by a short period of dizziness. Strangely enough, even though there were people around me, I felt they were very far from me. Call it daydreaming, but I am certain that I was reliving the moment when my father was taken from us. Though the day and time were never officially reported to us, I know that it was Saturday, April 29, 1972. The way I felt that day tells me so. How much I miss him!

Acknowledgements: I would like to acknowledge René Lemarchand, whose expertise and mentoring set me on the road of remembering for healing sake. I would also like to acknowledge my friend, Jodi Mikalachki, whose presence on the ground in Burundi and support encouraged me to tell my story, my brother and dear friend, Leonce Hakizimana, my husband Emmanuel, my daughter Nina, and my sons Herve and Bernard, for their unwavering support, encouragement, motivation, and most importantly, unconditional love. With heartfelt gratitude, I dedicate this work to all of you.

NOTES

1. Boniface Fidel Kiraranganya, *La vérité sur le Burundi: témoignage* (Sherbrooke, Québec: Éditions Naaman, 1985), 76.
2. René Lemarchand, "Le génocide de 1972 au Burundi: Les silences de l'Histoire," *Cahiers d'Études Africaines*, 42, Cahier 167, 2002, 551–67.
3. Ibid.
4. Ibid.
5. Ibrahim Omer, "Are Genetic Differences at Root of the Tutsi-Hutu Rwandan Conflict?" *Genetic Literacy Project*, 2013, Accessed at: http://www.geneticliteracyproject.org/2013/08/05/are-genetic-differences-at-the-root-of-the-tutsi-hutu-rwandan-conflict/#.U6hcX41dWpc.
6. Ibid.
7. Ibid.
8. I was one of the lucky few who passed a highly selective national test at the end of the sixth grade. I always knew I was privileged and never took it for granted. Putting a girl in school was against the norm, but my parents understood the value of education for their daughters as well as their sons.

9. This was a common, albeit unfair, practice (among the haves and have-nots) that my mother, mind you, a Tutsi, cancelled as soon as my father died. That's the kind of mother I have!

10. The only official name I had at that time was "Ntihirageza"; I didn't become "Jeanine" until I got baptized when I was fifteen. Tragically, my father did not know "Jeanine." His second wife's children could not get baptized at birth (the norm in the Catholic Church) since he skipped church when he got married to her. That was one of the punishments for not obeying church rules.

Chapter 3

Anti-Imperialist Rhetoric and Patterns of Genocide Denial in Zimbabwe

Chielozona Eze

The international definition of the crime of genocide is found in Articles II and III of the 1948 Convention on the Prevention and Punishment of Genocide adopted by the UN General Assembly on December 9, 1948. The convention understands genocide to mean any of the following acts committed with intent to destroy, in whole or in part, a national, ethnic, racial or religious group, such as (a) Killing members of the group; (b) Causing serious bodily or mental harm to members of the group; (c) Deliberately inflicting on the group conditions of life calculated to bring about its physical destruction in whole or in part; (d) Imposing measures intended to prevent births within the group.[1] Leo Kuper (1994) refines this definition by arguing that "the Convention definition of genocide may be summarized briefly as the intent to destroy *in whole or in part* a racial, religious, or national group *as such*, by killing members of the group or imposing conditions inimical to survival."[2]

Of importance in the above definition is the *intention* to destroy a group physically in whole or in part. Such intention is usually associated with the goal of eliminating or limiting the political, religious or economic influence or survival of that group. The above definition applies to many incidents of mass killings of members of particular ethnic groups by members of other ethnic groups in Africa. Such killings have the implicit goal of striking terror in the collective mind of the group. "In September 2010, the Gukurahundi massacres were classified as a genocide by the internationally recognised group Genocide Watch."[3] According to their report:

> In 1983 and 1984 massacres of over 20,000 Matabele citizens of Zimbabwe were committed by the Fifth Brigade of the Zimbabwe Army. These massacres are called the "Gukurahundi." This mass atrocity meets the definition of genocide because it targeted ethnic Matabele people. The massacres were carried

out by the North-Korean trained, exclusively Shona Fifth Brigade under orders from President Mugabe.[4]

The genocide in Zimbabwe involves the partial destruction or killing of members of an ethnic group. In March 1980, Robert Mugabe led Zimbabwe to independence with a solid victory in the country's first free national election. Since then he has had a firm grip on power. There are two easy explanations to his phenomenon of power control: (a) suppression of his opposition, the most violent of which was the already mentioned genocide; (b) crafty uses of anti-imperialist rhetoric as a means of self-justification, and denial of genocide and other instances of human rights abuses. My interest in this chapter is mainly in the latter, and to the degree that it demands a moral obligation to remember. It is horrifying enough that tens of thousands of innocent people lost their lives to one man's political ambition. Equally abhorrent is its denial, and this, I think, amounts to subjecting the dead to yet another form of death.

Indeed, the denial of genocide indirectly enhances and reinscribes the terror of the act in the consciousness of the survivors. The failure to acknowledge the genocide in Matabeleland has been exacerbated by Mugabe's influence and only now are we able to reconstruct its reach. What is framed within the language that draws on the *Gukurahundi* killings is essential to understanding the role not only of remembrance but also that of forgetting. It describes not only how the genocide is talked about but also the political impulses that erase the memory of the Zimbabwe genocide. Between this duality, history occupies a precarious place. In this chapter, I will endeavor to achieve three things: (a) discuss *Gukurahundi* as genocide; (b) analyze the crafty ways in which Robert Mugabe denies it; and (c) highlight the moral task of keeping the memory of genocide and other forms of human suffering alive in Africa.

GUKURAHUNDI

Gukurahundi is a Shona word, meaning the early rain that washes away the chaff before the spring rains. The initial report on the massacre of the innocent civilians in Matabeleland was produced by the Catholic Commission for Justice and Peace in Zimbabwe and the Legal Resources Foundation. It was later republished in South Africa by Jacana as *Gukurahundi*.[5] The publisher's note to the South African edition begins with a suggestive epigram: "'All of Gaul has been pacified'—Julius Caesar." *Gukurahundi* can be seen as a pacification of an unruly population by means of partial elimination. It seems to capture Robert Mugabe's mindset at the time when he ordered that the "chaff" of his revolution be washed away by the rain of the North Korean–trained 5th Brigade. To be sure, Robert Mugabe could not be said to be a bloodthirsty dictator. He was by no means comparable to Idi Amin. He did not just order the elimination of the members of the rival ethnic group, Ndebele. One has to understand the circumstances surrounding the unfortunate event. A little historical background may help our understanding in this regard.

The genocide in Zimbabwe was largely a product of an unfortunate chain of events. The country had just gained independence and was being sabotaged by the personnel from the former Rhodesian intelligence services, who connived with the apartheid South African government to destabilize Zimbabwe. More important than the continuous danger from South Africa were the remnants of animosity between the two major guerrilla armies, Zimbabwe People's Revolutionary Army (ZIPRA) (largely comprising Ndebele-speaking soldiers) and Zimbabwe African National Liberation Army (ZANLA) (largely Shona), and their political umbrella organizations, Zimbabwe African People's Union (ZAPU) (Joshua Nkomo, Ndebele) and the Zimbabwe African National Union – Patriotic Front (ZANU-PF) (Robert Mugabe, Shona). The unease between the two armies "and their respective political followings . . . played an incontrovertible role in the events of the 1980s."[6] These groups were not tribalist by nature and each of them recruited troops from Shona-speakers and Ndebele-speakers. Two things brought about the emergence of animosity between them. The first was the sabotage from the South African apartheid government that fed the two groups false information about each other's evil intent. The South African government successfully fanned the antagonism between Shona and Ndebele. The Ndebele were originally of the Khumalo clan; they broke away from their Zulu kindred in the 1820s and moved from the present day Kwazulu Natal. The Shona had nursed resentment against the Ndebele for the fact that they "defeated the Shona people of present day Zimbabwe and destroyed their cattle and livestock."[7] All the South African intelligence forces needed to do was keep the memory of the war between these ethnicities alive.

The second thing that fed the animosity between the two groups was the "complexity of integrating the two forces into one army after independence."[8] It might be argued that the first reason was the ultimate cause of the second. There had been some outbreaks of violence between ZIPRA and ZANLA. In an address in Bulawayo, Enos Nkala (Shona) was said to have warned ZAPU (Ndebele) that ZANU (Shona) would deliver a few blows to them. Whether Nkala referred to a metaphoric political blow or an actual military one was never clear. But it led to the Entumbane uprisings, during which ZIPRA and ZANLA fought a vicious battle for two days. Adding to the atmosphere of distrust was the apartheid South African-sponsored assassination attempt on Prime Minister Mugabe in August 1981 at Inkomo Barracks near Harare. The assassination attempt set the stage for the first rain of the season to wash away the chaff of the dissident forces; it gave Mugabe an excuse to go after his political adversaries who were easy to identify, as they were the other ethnicity. In that context

> the antagonism between the two guerilla armies hardened into hostilities between their political parties, as ZANU-PF became convinced that ZAPU was supporting a new dissident war in order to improve its standing in the country. ZAPU, in turn, has expressed its belief that ZANU-PF used the pretext of the disturbances as a long-awaited opportunity to crush ZAPU once and for all.[9]

The killing of more than 20,000 civilians in Matabeleland is therefore the result of a chain of unfortunate incidents, not an explosion of the so-called ancient tribal animosity, as the apartheid government or the members of the deposed Rhodesian white minority government would have the world believe. It was nonetheless a crime whose goal was to strike fear into the minds of the Ndebele ethnic group. It could be judged to be the result of Mugabe's paranoia about the members of the white minority government in South Africa and their former Rhodesian sympathizers.

Mugabe had entered into a contract with the government of North Korea to train a special army brigade, which was called the 5th Brigade. It was known for its brutality and it was unleashed on the population of Matabeleland. According to the report presented by the Catholic Commission for Justice and Peace, "over 20 000 people were killed by the 5th Brigade. These were innocent, unarmed civilians";[10] they were the "rubbish that was to be swept away."[11] Massacres occurred; rapes, beatings, torture, burnings, and deliberate starvation were the order of the day in Mugabe's attempt to stamp out opposition and eliminate the possibility of sabotage from South Africa or elsewhere.[12] The first official accusation of genocide came from Zimbabwe itself. According to Archbishop Pius Ncube, "Mugabe had a hidden agenda. The motive for these killings was to crush the people of Matabeleland so that they would conform to the ZANU-PF Government and give up their tribal identity and their attachment to ZAPU."[13] Judging from the archbishop's accusation, it seems evident that Mugabe's calculation was political and therefore premeditatedly genocidal. According to the definition of genocide given above, it is not just the number of casualties in mass killings that make it genocidal; it is largely the intention behind the killing. *Gukurahundi*, which was targeted at the opposition—members of a different ethnic group—is therefore genocide because of Mugabe's intent to destroy them, in part, for his own political goals.

CRAFTY USES OF ANTI-IMPERIALIST RHETORIC

Mugabe has not acknowledged that the killings in Matabeleland and elsewhere were acts of genocide. He has therefore not apologized.[14] The furthest he went in acknowledging it was his description of the killings as an act of madness. On the anniversary of the death of Joshua Nkomo, he said: "It was an act of madness, we killed each other and destroyed each other's property. . . . It was wrong and both sides were to blame."[15] Rather than admit to his intentional killing of the members of the opposing ethnic population, he went on to obfuscate his direct responsibility for the killing and for other instances of suppression of the opposition. In his denial of genocide and other instances of human rights abuses, he adopts the popular belief that the best defense is offense.

The government of Mugabe has succeeded in many ways in suppressing the remembrance of that genocide and other instances of human rights abuses; these include (1) blaming colonialists; and (2) blaming the victims who supposedly worked with the colonialists. All of this can be brought under the umbrella of his crafty manipulation of history and its symbols, that is, his uses of postcolonial imaginations. In some aspects of African politics and, to a large extent, cultural discourses, memory of the past is effectively translated into political capital. This owes in no small part to the fact that these discourses always presumed the gaze of the other, the West. The presence of the West is a constant reminder of what Chinua Achebe calls the African person's "wound in the soul."[16] The white man looms rather large in the African self-perception, and therefore the African must be literally on his guard all the time. Being on his guard allows him to subject the white man to a morally inferior position. Having put the white man in his place, the African categorically insulates himself against any opposition to his ideas. The African effectively toes a monological path in his world in the guise of being not like the colonial master or being authentically oneself. Whereas the colonial master deserves condemnation, the African leaders, who, as Fanon has noted, have merely occupied the posts vacated by the colonist, begin to replicate the ills of their former colonizers. They become uncontested leaders to whom their people owe limitless gratitude.[17]

In 1997, Robert Mugabe launched what he called the Third Chimurenga, meaning the third phase of Zimbabwe's revolutionary struggle. The First Chimurenga was the war of independence, also known as the Second Matabele War of 1896–1897. The Second Chimurenga was the Rhodesian Bush War or the Zimbabwe Liberation War, which lasted from 1966 to 1979. The Third Chimurenga was designed to achieve what the other two could not: the complete liberation of Zimbabwe from its colonial heritage. Mugabe understood himself as fulfilling the promises of the heroes of Africa's liberation struggles; this includes the Organization of African Unity (OAU), whose greatest success, according to him, "has been in orchestrating the complete decolonisation of Africa, much against violent opposition from colonial powers."[18] Addressing the OAU general assembly on the 40th anniversary of

Ghana's independence, he seized on this enviable success to hone his visions for Zimbabwe: "In Zimbabwe, and only because of the colour line arising from British colonialism, 70 percent of the best arable land is owned by less than one percent of the population who happen to be white, while the black majority are congested on barren land."[19]

Although not original in this way of thinking in Africa, Mugabe has heavily influenced its direction and helped entrench it in African political consciousness. He achieved this through his keen uses of postcolonial righteous anger. Take, for example, the most recent failed European and African Union summit for political and economic partnership in Lisbon in late 2007. There might have been some disagreement in the economic details that were discussed; however, the overarching narrative is how Mugabe hijacked the forum and brought other African leaders to bow to his anti-imperialist rhetoric, so that no meaningful dialogue could take place. According to reports, "friction over human rights records nagged at their attempt to seal a new alliance as leaders traded criticism, especially over Zimbabwean President Robert Mugabe."[20] Chancellor Angela Merkel of Germany concluded her sharp criticism of Mugabe's human rights abuses by arguing that "Zimbabwe concerns all of us, in Europe and in Africa."[21] *The New York Times* reported about the change of mood and, therefore, of the outcome of the discussion; this is because African countries closed ranks around Mugabe after the criticism from the West. "Senegal's president, Abdoulaye Wade, said that the comments about Mr. Mugabe were 'not true,' and that Mrs. Merkel was misinformed. Zimbabwe is making progress toward democracy, and should be helped, not sanctioned."[22] It is, of course, wrong to claim that Zimbabwe was making progress when Mugabe's police were cracking down on the opposition. Mugabe himself responded in his usual manner, claiming that the Europeans were just being Europeans; they were steeped in arrogance, having been influenced by Britain, the arch-colonizer, the evil imperialist. Europeans were only the mouthpiece of 10 Downing Street. In his words, "the colonial power continually manipulates us and wants to change the government, but we say no, we have the right to determine our own future. We will never be a colony again!"[23] One takes note of how he pulls the most important strings that would resonate with the African wound in the soul: "the colonial power," "our own future," and "never be a colony again."

Mugabe's culture of exclusion and the intimidation of his perceived enemies continued even decades after *Gukurahundi*. As Sabelo J. Ndlovu-Gatsheni argues:

> After the 2000 and 2002 elections, in which many people voted for the opposition Movement for Democratic Change (MDC) in the parliamentary and presidential elections, Mugabe began to divide Zimbabweans into traitors, puppets,

sell-outs, enemies of the nation versus patriots and authentic national subjects. This mentality enabled a politics of exclusion of a large number of people from the nation and the authorization of violence against those who were written out of the nation.[24]

Mugabe sustains his support not only by intimidating people but also by manipulating history and national symbols. Ndlovu-Gatsheni argues further that

> Mugabe has been one of the most charismatic African leaders. He is very eloquent and he has used these qualities effectively to deliver "fine speeches" to sway the masses and the world to his side. Populist-inspired speeches are often empty of content. This is true of Mugabeism which has mobilized race, culture, history and memory to advance its cause.[25]

His speeches provoked a torrent of emotion in his listeners and effectively turned memory into a tool of ideology. Mugabe's rhetoric is aimed at denying genocide for the same reason that the perpetrators of genocide everywhere deny it: denying genocide seeks to free the denier from moral and social responsibility toward the victims. Second, it helps the denier to maintain power.

AFRICAN MORAL CHALLENGES *OR* HOW MEMORY CAN SERVE HUMANITY

As Ndlovu-Gatsheni has stated, there are many traps in taking most backward-looking, nativist ideologies suggested by African nationalist leaders as alternatives to Western imperialism. He argues, for example, that "those reading Mugabeism as left-nationalism emphasize its rejection of neoliberal orthodoxy, opting for the pursuit of a heterodox economic plan."[26] But pitting such narrow left-nationalist ideology against the equally narrow and oppressive Western ideology risks perceiving Africans as pawns in an ideological game. Thus, the task of African intellectuals in this regard is to place the African subject at the center of every valuation; this includes discussions about the past. How should Africans engage with their past, which has ample instances of violence perpetrated by Africans against Africans? For one, harping on the structural and psychological devastations of colonialism can only make Africans engage with the moral challenges of living with one another.

Remembrance is not a value in itself and may be overly oppressive. In a Nietzschean vein, David Rieff suggests that society might be better off if people could choose to forget events rather than remember. Amnesia, he argues, would help temper people's desire for retaliation.[27] This is a rather controversial and a highly improbable position. It is fair to suggest that Rieff's notion of forgetting is a shared project with the sentiment of *Gukurahundi*. Forgetting could not be a way of resolving or reconciling the trauma of genocide because it is the continuation of its basic impulses. In this regard, therefore, forgetting becomes a secondary type of "washing away."

In the first place, the people affected cannot choose to remember or forget. People hardly forget traumatic events in their lives; to propose collective amnesia seems to be an indirect way of promoting selective remembering. Forgetting in the sense prescribed by Rieff is only a form of post-traumatic denial and nothing more. Selective remembering can, indeed, be more dangerous than collective, somewhat ritualized moments of memory. Selective remembering could easily become a moral tool to judge others as irredeemably evil. The more important question, however, is how to remember in order to heal the trauma of genocide, not how to defend forms of denial.

While it may be true that the dangers of the present may be caught in the winds of the past, and that this may spark further movements of mass violence, how we think of progress here is of great importance. How do we think of production of history as parallel with the moral needs of empathy? In Walter Benjamin's *On the Concept of History*, he makes use of Paul Klee's painting, *Angelus Novus*, to illustrate his lessons about the importance of memory.[28] In the painting, the angel is staring at something. It is as if he is distancing himself from what he is staring at. His eyes and mouth are open, and his wings are outstretched. For Benjamin, this is how the angel of history must look. "Where we see the appearance of a chain of events, he sees one single catastrophe, which unceasingly piles rubble on top of rubble and hurls it before his feet."[29] The angel would like to pause for a while in order to awaken the dead. "But a storm is blowing from Paradise, it has caught itself up in his wings and is so strong that the Angel can no longer close them. The storm drives him irresistibly into the future, to which his back is turned, while the rubble-heap before him grows sky-high. That which we call progress, is this storm."[30] Benjamin differentiates between two approaches to history. The first is that of historicism, which can be understood as a "commitment to a seamless narrative that plots ongoing efforts to carry forward" to a particular goal.[31] The second approach to history is historical materialism, which underscores the present: "History is the subject of a structure whose site is not homogenous, empty time, but time filled by the presence of the now [*Jetztzeit*]."[32] As Patrick Hutton observes, "the 'now-time' (*Jetztzeit*) is the point of departure for any critical assessment of the meaning of events out of the past."[33] A historical materialist view of history admits to the impossibility of recording the past as it really happened—contrary to what the adherents of historicism would allege. This does not mean that all details in the past do not matter. They do. But they reveal themselves in flashes, especially in relation to the *Jetzt*. For the benefit of the present, it is absolutely necessary that one seizes each flash of memory.[34]

The fact that memory reveals itself in flashes shows that it is fragile. The chronicler of history, in Benjamin's view, engages with empathy either to strengthen the present according to the vision of predecessors or to free it from the stranglehold of the past. The heirs of the ruling class write with empathy for their ancestors, whose lives and actions that established the status quo are interpreted as heritage. With attention to the material conditions of people, the historical materialist, in contrast, contemplates with horror the world that the ruling class interprets as cultural heritage, and acknowledges that that world "owes its existence not only to the toil of the great geniuses, who created it, but also to the nameless drudgery of its contemporaries . . . He regards it as his task to brush history against the grain."[35] Thus, the historical materialist also views history with empathy, but only for the dispossessed, for the benefit of those suffering now.

Michael Löwy explains the importance of taking up memory in the moment of danger. It is to "show presence of mind (*Geistesgegenwart*) to grasp the unique moment, this fleeting precarious opportunity of salvation (*Rettung*) before it is too late."[36] Benjamin critiques Marx's exclusively materialist interpretation of history and emphasizes the importance of the spiritual elements in the struggle such as "confidence, courage, humour, cunning and fortitude."[37] Thus, in the Marxist spirit, the goal of remembrance is to change the present for the benefit of the underprivileged; it is not to punish the privileged. Confidence, courage, humor, love, and fortitude seek to restore fairness on the face of the earth, and they do this in addition to the fact that the memory which they accompany appears in flashes. In short every remembrance of the past must be accompanied by the spiritual elements and the humility that comes with the awareness of the fragility of memory. If memory is fragile, then it is a contradiction to seek to make it absolute. One makes memory absolute by subjecting it to the service of an ideology.

We thus return to the moral impulses behind the injunction to fight genocide denial, the injunction to remember. We remember in order to keep the ugly incident of the past from repeating. In line with Benjamin's thinking, keeping the memory of the past becomes a moral imperative, for it helps to prevent the emergence of a new ideology. If *Gukurahundi* means "washing away," which, as we have shown above, implies forgetting, remembrance means its opposite in a particular sense: what has been washed away returns to the shores of our moral consciousness. Memory brings back the dignity of those who have been washed away. Bringing the memory of the victims of genocide back to our memory has an added advantage of conferring dignity on our own lives. It may prevent thoughts of genocide in the future.

NOTES

1. "Convention on the Prevention and Punishment of the Crime of Genocide," Accessed at: https://www.oas.org/dil/1948_Convention_on_the_Prevention_and_Punishment_of_the_Crime_of_Genocide.pdf.
2. Leo Kuper, "Theoretical Issues Relating to Genocide: Uses and Abuses," in *Genocide: Conceptual and Historical Dimensions*, ed. G. Andreopoulos (Philadelphia, PA: University of Pennsylvania Press, 1994), 34.
3. "The *Gukurahundi* Massacres, 1983–1987: Breaking the Silence Report," *The Mike Campbell Foundation*, Accessed at: http://www.mikecampbellfoundation.com/page/the-gukurahundi-massacres.
4. Ibid.
5. "The Catholic Commission for Justice and Peace," *Gukurahundi in Zimbabwe: A Report on the Disturbances in Matabeleland and the Midlands 1980–1988* (Johannesburg, South Africa: Jacana Media, 2007).
6. Ibid., 45.
7. "Matabele wars 1836–1896," *South African History Online: A Peoples' History*, Accessed at: http://www.sahistory.org.za/south-africa-1806-1899/matabele-wars-1836-1896.
8. "The Catholic Commission," 46.
9. Ibid., 46–47.
10. Ibid., xi.
11. Martin Meredith, *Our Votes, Our Guns: Robert Mugabe and the Tragedy of Zimbabwe* (New York, NY: Public Affairs, 2002), 66.
12. See also Peter Godwin, *When a Crocodile Eats the Sun: A Memoir of Africa* (New York, NY: Little Brown and Company, 2006), for a more intimate account of Mugabe's violent oppression of the opposition.
13. "The Catholic Commission," xi.
14. A part of this section appears in a somewhat different format in Chielozona Eze, *Postcolonial Imagination and Moral Representations in African Literature and Culture* (Lanham, MD: Lexington Books, 2011).
15. "Mugabe: Madness of Matabele Deaths," *British Broadcasting Company* (BBC), July 2, 2000, Accessed at: http://news.bbc.co.uk/2/hi/africa/816129.stm. See also http://www.zambiawatchdog.com/mugabe-set-to-face-charges-of-genocide/.
16. Chinua Achebe, "The Novelist as a Teacher," in *Hopes and Impediments: Selected Essays* (New York: Anchor, 1988), 44–45.
17. Frantz Fanon, *The Wretched of the Earth*, trans. C. Farrington (London: Penguin Books, 1967).
18. Robert Mugabe, *The Third Chimurenga: Inside the Third Chimurenga* (Department of Information and Publicity, Office of the President & Cabinet, 2001), 17.
19. Ibid., 26.
20. "Europe, Africa Seek New Relationship at Summit," *Associated News*, January 30, 2008, Accessed at: www.iht.com/articles/ap/2007/12/08/europe/EU-GEN-EU-Africa-Summit.php.

21. Ibid.

22. See Stephen Castle, "Mugabe's Presence Hijacks European-African Meeting," *The New York Times*, December 9, 2007, Accessed at: www.nytimes.com/2007/12/09/world/africa/09summit.html.

23. See "Mugabe Responds to European Critics," December 9th, 2007, Accessed at: www.enews20.com/news_Mugabe_Responds_to_European_Critics_04339.html.

24. Sabelo J. Ndlovu-Gatsheni, "Making Sense of Mugabeism in Local and Global Politics: 'So Blair, Keep your England and Let me keep my Zimbabwe,'" *Third World Quarterly*, 30, (6), 2009, 1139–58, p. 1140.

25. Ibid., 1142.

26. Ibid., 1143.

27. Rieff, *Against Remembrance*.

28. I have explored Walter Benjamin more extensively in Chielozona Eze, *Race, Decolonization, and Global Citizenship* (Rochester, NY: University of Rochester Press, 2018).

29. Walter Benjamin, "On the Concept of History," in *Walter Benjamin: Selected Writings, Vol. 4, 1938–1940*, ed. H. Eiland and M. Jennings (Cambridge, MA: The Belknap Press of Harvard University Press, 2006).

30. Ibid.

31. Patrick Hutton, "Walter Benjamin: The Consolation of History in a Paris Exile," *Historical Reflections*, 36, (1), 2010, 76–94, p. 86.

32. Benjamin, "On the Concept of History," 395.

33. Hutton, "Walter Benjamin," 86.

34. Benjamin, "On the Concept of History," Thesis VI, 391.

35. Ibid.

36. Michael Löwy, *Fire Alarm: Reading Walter Benjamin's On the Concept of History* (London: Verso, 2005), 44.

Click here to enter text.

37. Benjamin, "On the Concept of History," Thesis IV, 390.

Chapter 4

American Slavery, the New Jim Crow, and Genocide

Lissa Skitolsky

At this critical moment in American politics, we are still working through the fact that on June 1, 2020, the federal government marshaled officers from the Secret Service, the United States Park Police, National Guard, Capitol Police, the Bureau of Alcohol, Tobacco, Firearms and Explosives, the Marshal's Service, the Bureau of Prisons, Customs and Border Protection and Immigration and Customs Enforcement in order to attack peaceful protestors with tear gas and flash bomb grenades to clear a path for the president to take his picture in front of a church, awkwardly holding a bible with his trademark smirk. This use of unprovoked state violence against citizens who gathered to insist that Black Lives Matter was not seen or reported as a crime—but it says everything about the connection between genocide and the history of slavery in the United States.

The collective inability to see state violence as criminal violence is made possible by the obscuring of this violence through the lens of our neoliberal sensibility that sees anti-Black violence as an exception to the norm of our just justice system, and through the lens of our post-racial sensibility that regards systemic racial terror as a problem of the American past, overcome in the present. The international protests on behalf of Black lives in the aftermath of George Floyd's murder have forced a long overdue moment of global reckoning with the systemic, lethal harms of institutional anti-Black violence that cannot be *seen* or *taken seriously* by the neoliberal and post-racial sensibility of the American present. Specifically, this global reckoning has entailed a new willingness to examine how anti-Black violence is inflicted and enforced by every social and political institution, by our national narratives and monuments, and by our disciplines and modes of knowledge acquisition. It is also imperative for white genocide scholars to reckon with the racist presuppositions that inform the nature and the categories of our analysis, and that have served to perpetually defer attention away from systemic anti-Black violence in our own countries as outside-of or unrelated-to our concern with past events of genocide that consume our attention and verify our definitions. As succinctly explained by Joy James in her book, *Resisting State Violence: Radicalism, Gender, and Race in U.S. Culture:* "Like a catch-22 situation, the more one memorializes genocide in past atrocities, the more opaque the concept may become in contemporary political life."[1]

In our effort to reckon with the exclusion of systemic anti-Black violence from the academic interest and concern of white genocide scholars, we must consider the methodology of comparative genocide studies that proceeds by way of viewing one or two historical examples of a state-sanctioned massacre as paradigmatic of our understanding of genocide, against which all other episodes of mass state violence are judged as more or less genocidal. In scholarship and popular discourse, it is evident that the Holocaust has always been viewed as the ultimate paradigm of genocide, beyond question and incomparable to other genocides. Yehuda Bauer illustrates and summarizes this view in his sentiment on this issue in that there is no precedent for a Holocaust in human history.[2] Likewise, the well-worn catchphrase in reference to Holocaust remembrance—Never Again—reinforces the singularity of the Holocaust insofar as this phrase suggests the Holocaust's incomparability to contemporary forms of state-sanctioned, genocidal violence.

Why does the Holocaust act as a guiding principle or standard in comparative genocide studies? In what way does such a conceptualization, such a starting point, control or distort the comparative analysis? The term "genocide" is both a legal and moral term and occupies a distinctive place in our political imaginary as the very worst violence that a state can inflict on its citizenry. It is a model of the *most extreme* form of crime that a state can inflict against its people, but a Holocaust-centric view also serves to rationalize *other* state-sanctioned atrocities in the past and present that do not *measure up* to the form and brutality of the Nazi genocide in our political imaginary. For this reason, we must examine the role that the Holocaust-centric view of genocide plays in the economy of anti-Black violence endemic to the contemporary sociopolitical order that is seen and assessed as *less than* criminal or systemic, and as "less than" genocide proper. In this chapter, I argue that we can only start to grasp the political significance of the traditional view of the Holocaust as *a singular event* (reinforced by the methodology of genocide studies) when we consider how scholars make use of the presupposition of its singularity in order to defend the long-standing, trenchant distinction between American slavery and genocide. This distinction plays such an outsized role in our political imaginary and in our neoliberal and post-racial sensibility of the American present that for most established, white, Western scholars who work in the field of Holocaust and genocide studies it simply doesn't *make sense* to discuss or imagine the history of anti-Black genocide in the United States.

The exclusion of American slavery from genocide studies is problematic because it indicates that American slavery is a political atrocity that cannot be thought of as on par with other sovereign efforts to destroy other populations also marked by race and class. This disavowal cannot be explained in terms of paradigmatic thinking alone but is also supported by other false assumptions that have nevertheless informed research in comparative genocide studies. Through critical analysis of traditional assumptions about the Holocaust that have secured it a singular place in our political imaginary, I hope to better expose the fissure between imagination and fact that has precluded the analysis of American slavery as a system of genocide. This is a critical task for the present, for the way we imagine the facts of the Holocaust and American slavery in our political imaginary serves to support the neoliberal and post-racial sensibility of anti-Black violence that reinforces white indifference to the repetition of anti-Black genocide in the American present. In particular, the genocidal wounds inflicted by our penal system—this new Jim Crow—are justified as justice as opposed to a system of senseless violence that continues to destroy communities marked by race and class.

Instead of simply rejecting the Holocaust as the paradigm of genocide, I detail the false assumptions that have historically served to justify the sharp distinction between genocide and American slavery. First, I focus on the pragmatic arguments for this distinction and argue that it is no longer possible to sustain the view that the Nazi Holocaust—unlike American slavery—was entirely non-pragmatic. Second, I illustrate that it is not possible to identify the essence of either the Holocaust or the Atlantic slave trade as mass murder or slave labor. Finally, I demonstrate the infeasibility of comparing the intent of the Nazis and the intent of American slave owners in an effort to discern whether the Atlantic slave trade was genocidal. Against this traditional approach that defines genocide from the perspective of the perpetrators, I support the effort of Claudia Card to define genocide in terms of the distinct harms it inflicts on its victims. I argue that if we adopt Card's view of genocide as the infliction of social death against a targeted group, then we can recognize the centrality of American slavery to any genealogy of genocidal practices. To be clear, chattel slavery is not *like* genocide. *American slavery was a system of anti-Black genocide* that has been perpetuated through different historical forms of state-sanctioned racial terror against African Americans, justified and normalized through cultural assumptions about Blacks, and provides the basis of the era of mass incarceration.

Further, I argue that the false distinction between American slavery and genocide serves at least three nefarious political aims. First, in the literature, the distinction sustains a false narrative about the American Dream that rests on racist judgments about African Americans. Second, because it relies on embedded racist assumptions, it also allows Americans to disavow the evolution of genocidal violence in the United States against African Americans. Third, it serves to perpetuate the racist structure of the criminal justice system in the United States that targets Black communities and destroys the vitality of African American families. Thus, our denial of the American genocide against African slaves has led to the *return of the repressed* in the form of mass incarceration and general indifference about state violence against Black and Brown bodies. African Americans are still seen and imagined as inherently *criminal* rather than as unnaturally vulnerable to police brutality and state-sanctioned torture and murder. Central to this sensibility—and the normalization of state violence against Black communities as such—is the view that American anti-Black racism has never been *genocidal*, even if it produces mass atrocities. As James explains, this default disavowal of the genocidal character of American racism accounts for "the semi-illiteracy of conventional rhetoric shaping the dominant discourse on race," that "arises from severing racism from its logical culmination in genocide and from restricting the referent for human atrocities to past holocausts that have been commodified for mass consumption as historical objects and moral reminders." James also insists that "The moral import of racism is virtually meaningless after it has been severed from genocide."[3]

In order to meet this historical moment, we must insist—against the tradition—that the violence that links American slavery to mass incarceration be characterized as genocide and not simply as mass atrocities. Genocide serves to name both a system of violence and the senselessness of this violence; it designates that which need not and should not have occurred, and the moral outrage that ought to accompany its continuance. The default exclusion of chattel slavery from the history of genocide—the impossibility of its appearance—is what we must confront if we are to honor and listen to the testimonies of African Americans rather than continue to exclude them and deny them any authority in thinking-through the genocidal violence in the American present inflicted by an administration that has embraced white supremacy with impunity.

THE HOLOCAUST AND OUR POLITICAL IMAGINARY

The popular distinction between American slavery and genocide is reinforced in the field of Holocaust and comparative genocide studies through the exclusion of American slavery by definition. If genocide scholars do consider slavery in relation to genocide, they often claim that slavery is a form of *cultural* genocide as opposed to *real*, or *physical* genocide. This distinction is defended on the basis of the intent specific to genocide, understood as a state-sanctioned attack on a specific ethnic, religious, racial, or national group, *as such*. Thus, *only* if the intent of the perpetrators is to destroy the *enemy* as a desired end in itself, does the attack constitute genocide. If the perpetrators hope to profit from the destruction of the targeted population through the accumulation of wealth or land or the acquisition of power, then we assume that their intent is not for the destruction of the targeted population "as such"; in this case, their attack does not constitute genocide.

As the case of American slavery shows, the fallout of this understanding is operative in the most pernicious ways. For example, Bauer argues that the Holocaust was unprecedented because it was completely non-pragmatic.[4] Likewise, in his influential essay on "Conceptual Constraints on Thinking about Genocide" in which he argues *against* the use of paradigmatic thinking in comparative genocide studies, David Moshman still takes it as self-evident that American slavery would be excluded from a study of comparative genocides because killing and cultural destruction were not the primary intent.[5] These offhand remarks illustrate the role that the Holocaust plays in our political imaginary as a way of framing what suffering is considered and known as such and what is not. For they cannot be rationally defended, and depend upon a false narrative about the Nazi genocide in which the economic importance of slave labor in the Jewish ghettos and concentration camps—and the utility of the genocide for the German economy—is selectively read out or viewed as irrelevant to the larger political and historical significance of the Holocaust.

Alternatively, the system of American slavery occupies a role in our political imaginary that reduces it entirely to a utilitarian system necessary for a new nation, despite the fact that American slaves were often worked to death, tortured, raped, and/or killed by their masters. We ignore the utilitarian features of the Holocaust just as we ignore the excessive cruelty, terror, and murder that characterized American slavery in order to sustain their distinct roles *as* systems of suffering known (respectively) as *genocide* and *less than genocide* in our political imaginary. However, if we imagine the rapid extermination of Jews as the genuine expression of the Holocaust, then we can also imagine the slow death of millions of Blacks as the genuine expression of slavery. What we cannot do is understand why these systems of destruction occupy different roles in our political imaginary with reference to the historical facts.

The view of American slavery as informed by purely utilitarian concerns serves to justify the abduction, torture, and destruction of the enslaved peoples as a *necessary evil* in the teleological progression of the United States into a global power. Similarly, A. Dirk Moses explains in his article, "Conceptual Blockages and Definitional Dilemmas in the 'Racial Century':

Genocide of Indigenous Peoples and the Holocaust," that the distinction between *pragmatic* state violence and *non-pragmatic* genocidal violence interprets European imperialism and colonialism—made possible by the systematic destruction of indigenous populations—in a Hegelian vein as a necessary, inevitable course of events for the sake of cultural progress.[6] In this sense the distinction between (the utility of) American slavery and (the senselessness of) the Nazi genocide allows us to assimilate the former into a Hegelian narrative of historical progress as an unfortunate, but understandable, episode of moral callousness on behalf of our (otherwise magnanimous) founding fathers.

However, at the same time, this distinction is rarely defended but rather accepted as an epistemic starting point for inquiry, as a premise that grounds the historical study of genocides over time. For example, even though Moses problematizes the distinction between a *pragmatic* and a *non-pragmatic* genocide so as to better understand the slaughter of Native Americans as genocide (still a contested topic in the field), he also excludes any mention of slavery from his discussion of American genocide. His analysis is a reflection of the fact that even when white scholars offer expansive definitions of genocide, meant to encourage nontraditional, comparative analyses, they—almost involuntarily—exclude American slavery from their more inclusive genealogy of possible genocides. Their inability to think about chattel slavery as a system of anti-Black genocide—despite their recent "turn" toward colonialism—indicates that at stake is not simply how we record the past but how we read and understand our role in the present.

PRAGMATIC GOALS AND USELESS SUFFERING

What is the difference between American slavery and the Holocaust as systems of oppression? In the tradition of Holocaust and genocide studies, scholars have approached this question by following one of two directions for analysis: (a) discrediting one as genocide or (b) determining whose genocide caused the most suffering or impairment. This approach presupposes the framework for comparative genocide studies as a zero-sum game whereby the Jewish Holocaust was a "real" genocide only if American slavery was not. However, this framework only makes sense if we have already presupposed the singularity of the Holocaust as what is already at stake in the comparison. However, as I illustrated in the previous section, our presupposition that the Holocaust is "singular" in Western history has far-reaching effects on how we think and see genocide and state-sanctioned violence in general.

Departing from these lines of inquiry, there are two alternative ways we could approach the comparison between American slavery and the Holocaust.

First, we can address how their comparison emerges in the difference between the reception and analysis of American slavery and the Holocaust in academic and popular discourse. Second, we can also analyze the difference between how we understand anti-Semitism and anti-Black racism. I focus on the former in order to help explain our passive acceptance of anti-Black racism in the United States.

Early historical scholarship about the Nazi genocide, by scholars such as Steven T. Katz, Lucy Davidowitz, and Bauer, emphasized that the Jewish Holocaust was unprecedented because American slavery was to some extent justified or "understandable" in accord with pragmatic aims. For example, Bauer defends the claim that the Nazi genocide was unprecedented in light of its non-pragmatic intent to destroy the Jewish people as a goal in itself. He claims that the Nazis "did not kill the Jews in order to get their property. They took their property because they wanted, at first, to get rid of them, and then they robbed them on the way to killing them."[7] But how can Bauer make a gross generalization about the order of every Nazi's priorities as being to first kill Jews, and then to loot their possessions and property? There is no evidence to support this sweeping claim, which rests on proving the main psychological motive for hatred and/or indifference to the Jews for every ordinary German in the Nazi Reich. His claim rests on a certain model of moral psychology that holds that we always act in accord with a singular motive and intent that justifies our action to ourselves *before we act*.

The way that scholars frame the question of intent to distinguish between *genocidal* and *non-genocidal* violence is itself based on an anachronistic model of moral psychology that cannot account for the phenomenon of what Hannah Arendt referred to as *thoughtlessness*, or the inability and/or refusal to evaluate the moral worth of one's actions in order to carry on with business as usual (viz. "I just followed orders"). Bauer's contention that the Germans intended to *kill first* and *rob second* ignores how moral psychology is shaped and/or distorted by specifically *genocidal* relations of power that merge the individual will with the collective will through the sociopolitical organization of an entire nation to marginalize, degrade, and destroy populations marked by class, race, ethnicity, gender, and ability. It is more likely that many Germans were *thoughtless* and did not, in fact, rank the priority of killing versus robbing while participating in the general exploitation and destruction of the Jews, which had become an ordinary state of affairs.

I do not think it is possible to evaluate the *intent* of ordinary Germans as they plundered the homes of their Jewish neighbors, nor contrast the supposedly ideological motivations of Germans with the "pragmatic" motivations of American slave owners. For apart from the phenomenon of thoughtlessness that precludes any universal statement about perpetrator motivations, it is also not the case that we can easily distinguish between *pragmatic* and *ideological* motives. For intentions and actions are never purely pragmatic or ideological; instead, we act in a general context of what it is possible to think and what it is possible to do, where thought and action delimit and reinforce one another. This is a postmodern insight that arose from the effort to debunk the myth of *pure reason* that could operate in isolation of the network of power relations that coerce and produce language games and the institutions in which they operate. The view that some must perish so that others may flourish was operative in both American slavery and the Holocaust; this view is neither wholly pragmatic nor ideological.

Alternatively, the purported *usefulness* of a particular state policy masks or allows us to disavow the senseless violence it allows for. Thus, viewing American slavery as having been *useful* for the economy allows us to disavow the gratuitous amount of torture and murder on which it was based. We see this pattern in the present, as we view the prison system (falsely) as useful for public safety, so that we can disavow the excessive violence and torture inflicted on citizens and non-citizens in prisons and detention centers. Oppressive networks of power relations are not inevitable, but we reify them through interpreting the suffering of the powerless as meaningful in itself, as necessary for the health and progress of those with social, economic, and political power. The distinction between slavery as having a *pragmatic* function and genocide as lacking any practical function simply re-inscribes the racist logic that the abduction and destruction of Africans was *necessary* for white progress.

In the past decade, Holocaust scholars have illustrated the pragmatic dimensions of the Nazi genocide by positioning it within the larger history of colonialism, imperialism, and capitalism—or the effort of the nation-state to accelerate its ability to compete in the global economy. Furthermore, in his book, *Hitler's Beneficiaries*, Holocaust historian Götz Aly illustrates that the desire for material well-being motivated ordinary Germans to support Nazis, and shows the extent to which ordinary Germans enjoyed their new prosperity at the expense of their neighbors.[8] Though historians have previously revealed the extent to which German and American industries profited from the Nazi genocide, Aly is the first to focus on the importance of economic motives in the popular support for the Third Reich among both Nazis and ordinary German citizens. The Nazi state solved the crisis of unemployment through the destruction of its Jewish citizens, and Germans were willing to look the other way in order to profit from their plunder. Likewise, in his book, *Black Earth*, Timothy Snyder presents another dimension of the pragmatic character of the Nazi genocide by arguing that Hitler promoted the destruction of other national groups in the milieu of an ecological panic to ensure that Germans could flourish amidst a scarcity of natural resources.[9] All of these recent studies serve to throw doubt on Bauer's claim that the Holocaust is *unprecedented* in light of its *non-pragmatic* nature, and so also throw doubt on a primary justification for the theoretical distinction between American slavery and genocide as two "different" systems of oppression. This distinction is a relic of an obsolete theory of moral psychology based on the fiction of our capacity for pure reason separate and apart from practical thought, which can thereby motivate action on a purely ideological basis separate and apart from pragmatic aims. Lastly, the view of the Holocaust as entirely non-pragmatic rests on viewing the Atlantic slave trade as entirely pragmatic and thus necessary for cultural progress. This view whitewashes the excessive cruelty and useless violence that characterized the American slave trade.

In the next section, I argue that our refusal to recognize the distinctly genocidal structure of anti-Black violence in the United States has played an essential role in the economy of genocidal practices over time. This refusal is essential to the neoliberal and post-racial sensibility of the American present—reinforced by our public and professional discourse—that serves to perpetually defer the fact of systemic anti-Black violence with reference to a norm that has never existed, or an American system of justice that does not serve to target Black citizens *as such* for suspicion, arrest, torture, incarceration and murder. The entrenched discursive distinction between American slavery and genocide supports this deferral insofar as Americans have never had to reckon with slavery *as* genocide, and so cannot recognize the transmutation of genocidal policies over time. Instead, since the formal eras of slavery and Jim Crow have come to an end, most Americans believe that our public policies are not based on a legal structure of discrimination and persecution. Michelle Alexander refers to mass incarceration as "the new Jim Crow" to emphasize how this system has served to perpetuate the racist logic of the Jim Crow laws and similarly serves to continue patterns of state-sanctioned violence toward Blacks in ways that minimize how this violence is seen as part of our moral consideration.[10] However, when we consider the historical conditions of confinement, in addition to the disproportionate number of Black men who are imprisoned and killed, then we can better grasp how slavery, Jim Crow, and mass incarceration are different forms of state violence in a continuous history of American genocide against Africans and African Americans.

THE BANALITY OF GENOCIDE: SLAVERY AS AN AMERICAN INSTITUTION

The difference between the crimes of mass murder and genocide does not lie in body count, but rather the mode of destruction. The crime of mass murder does not entail the targeting of individuals as members of larger communities already excluded from moral consideration and the protection of the law. It refers instead to the act of killing a large number of people in a short span of time. And so, those who commit murder do not aim to make the lives and deaths of their victims *indecent* as a *method* of destruction, as their aim is fulfilled in the moment of committing their crime. On the other hand, those who commit genocide do not aim for the immediate destruction of a large group of people, but instead for the ongoing destruction of an entire community for the sake of total domination. For this reason, genocidal regimes aim to degrade the quality of their victims' lives, as opposed to merely killing a particular quantity of people. This is necessary in order for genocide to inflict transgenerational wounds that prevent entire communities from participating in social relations and rituals that make life meaningful, or that allow communities to establish life as meaningful and purposeful. Card coopted the term "social death" from Orlando Patterson's work on American slavery in order to signify the form of this degradation, or *how* states are able to undermine the vitality of entire communities.

Although Card adopted the term "social death" to name the distinct harm of genocide and to identify its specific brand of evil, she never drew out the obvious implication that American slavery itself, then, represents a genocide rather than a *different* form of state violence with some legal and/or moral justification.[11] Social death describes the effect of genocide or how it affects its victims; it refers to the collective loss of rituals, symbols, songs, stories, and generational ties that once made life meaningful. When a community suffers from social death, then death itself—bereft of elegiac rituals—becomes indecent. So, for example, there was a distinct sort of harm suffered by Jews who died in gas chambers. The harm of their profane deaths is irreducible to the harm of their murder. Analogously, there was a distinct harm suffered by Africans who died in the course of the Middle Passage, chained to the bottom of a ship. And there was a distinct harm suffered by slaves when they witnessed their children treated as the property of others, to be harmed and sold at whim.

The rationale behind the traditional view that American slavery was *pragmatic* while the Holocaust was *non-pragmatic* is based on the false assumption that since slaves were valued as property, they were "taken care of" to an extent that the Jewish slaves of Auschwitz were not. This view is expressed by Hannah Arendt in *The Origins of Totalitarianism*, when she writes, "Throughout history slavery has been an institution within a social order; slaves were not, like concentration-camp inmates, withdrawn from the sight and hence the protection of their fellow-men; as instruments of labor they had a definite price and as property a definite value."[12] Historians portray the labor in the Nazi camp as a prelude to physical death by exhaustion or disease, whereas they portray the lives of American slaves as possessing a modicum of security and health. In reality, the lives of American slaves were no more secure than the lives of Jews in Nazi Germany, and their value as commodities did not serve to guarantee a modicum of safety, dignity, or health.

The view that American plantation owners *took care of* their slaves follows from the popular romanticization of American slavery and the Southern plantation. In reality, American slavery was enforced through a gratuitous amount of brutal violence whose sadism far outstripped its utilitarian value. Of course, the reality is hard to square with the image of the well-meaning Christian plantation owner, and it threatens to disrupt the patriotic nostalgia for the wisdom of our founding fathers. The denial of the real conditions of American slavery (reinforced by the traditional distinction between "slavery" and "genocide") also allows us to ignore and deny the centrality of genocidal violence to the founding and structure of the United States. This prevents us from inquiring into the historical transmutation of genocidal violence against racialized populations in the United States, and prevents our ability to see or care about how African Americans in the *present* are still subject to the same exploitative, racist system of genocide that characterizes the American *past*.

And yet this view is only possible if we ignore or reject the epistemic value of all testimony, texts, aesthetic works and histories by African Americans that attest to the ways in which the genocidal logic of chattel slavery was re-produced in the historical forms of Jim Crow, spectacle lynching, and prison labor. And indeed, we can trace the historical refusal of scholars in the field of Holocaust and genocide studies to consider American anti-Black violence as genocidal—as targeting Black communities *as such*—to their rejection and dismissal of the 1951 report *We Charge Genocide: The Crime of Government Against the Negro People* presented by the Civil Rights Congress (CRC) when they became the first group in history to make use of the UN Convention Against Genocide in order to file a petition against the United States.[13] The aim of this petition was to formally charge the United States of the (new) crime of genocide for the institutional and systematic destruction and economic exploitation of Black communities. At the time it was presented, the UN refused to take up the petition or consider the analysis and evidence provided by Black scholars, activists, politicians, lawyers and artists about the genocidal character of anti-Black racism in the United States. Their refusal to hear the petition was followed by Raphaël Lemkin's indignant refusal to take it seriously, and these two refusals informed the sensibility of genocide in academic and popular culture that is marked by limits that prevent us from thinking, imagining, or perceiving the possibility of American genocide. These limits also prevent us from thinking about the systemic anti-Black violence operative in the historical systems of slavery, Jim Crow, spectacle lynching, and incarceration as *genocidal* violence that aims to destroy Black communities *as such*. Despite its historical importance, the *We Charge Genocide* petition remains a largely unexamined founding text for genocide scholarship.

The CRC's demand for international recognition of the distinctly *genocidal* violence perpetrated by Jim Crow laws in the United States between 1890 and 1965 was a direct political critique of its institutions. It was also a demand that the American destruction of Black communities be seen as an event and as a pattern within history that marks the severity and structure of the anti-Black violence that has been embedded in US law and society in the past and present. The conveners of the petition intentionally used the term "genocide" because they explained that it is necessary to oppose the "pious phrases" and "deadly legal euphemisms" that mask the regularity and brutality of state-sanctioned violence against Black Americans. They argue that without this term to describe the system of anti-Black violence in the United States, we are not able to actually confront the crime and the violence itself as it is experienced. In the same vein, when underground rappers insisted on using the terms "genocide" and "holocaust" to describe the nature and effects of the American Criminal Justice system, they take up the mission of the now defunct CRC insofar as they similarly believe in the political importance of the term "genocide" to contest the disarticulation of systemic violence against Black communities in American discourse and white sensibility.

Central to every genocide is the murder of the family or the denial of a population's *right* to familial and fraternal bonds. American slavery was a system of genocide because it was based on the destruction of familial ties and the exploitation of entire families. The entire economy of American slavery was based on the repeated murder of family units: from the original abduction of individuals to the rape of female slaves in order to sell their children, to the separation of families on the "selling block," slavery was based on the continuous destruction and exploitation of family units. And the systematic, state-directed effort to destroy Black families and weaken intergenerational bonds in Black communities did not end with the Thirteenth Amendment to the United States Constitution that formally abolished slavery in 1865. Instead, as Ava DuVernay illustrates in her critically acclaimed documentary "13th," the amendment's clause that allows for involuntary servitude as legal punishment has perpetuated the logic and harms of slavery through the criminalization and incarceration of millions of Black men who live under conditions *designed* to inflict mental and physical pain and sever family bonds.

Our inability to conceive of punishment in any terms other than the state-sanctioned infliction of pain is a testament to the poverty of our moral imagination. It also provides a clue about the historical importance of the category of the *criminal* to the efficient functionality of genocidal practices. In the United States, slavery was sustained by the creation of legislation that gave slave owners the right to use corporal punishment against their slaves as well as to kill them. In order to sustain the absolute power of white citizens over their slaves, a series of laws were passed to affect the legal *criminalization of Black life*, or through criminalizing basic capacities, such as reading, writing, agency, and movement, until there was always already a provocation for punitive punishment. Thus, in its origins, the US criminal justice system largely served to legalize a system of white supremacy through the exploitation of Africans and the destruction of their families. Their exploitation was first achieved through chattel slavery and justified with reference to racist ideology; now it is achieved through slave labor in the prisons and justified with reference to crime and punishment. In this way, the cognitive erasure of American slavery as a traumatic system of genocide allows for its historical repetition through the state-sanctioned infliction of traumatic suffering in our penal system that is *also* rendered invisible as a *necessary evil* rather than as the contemporary form of American genocide.

THE PENAL SYSTEM, SOCIAL DEATH, AND GENOCIDE

Although the recent media attention given to the obscenely high number of prisoners in the United States is a heartening development for social justice, the discussion threatens to avert our attention from the true moral atrocity of the prison system, or the everyday conditions of confinement that inflict excessive amounts of mental and physical pain upon our prisoner population. The conditions of confinement in the United States degrade and destroy the quality of our prisoners' lives. Central to the notion of genocide, or people-destruction, is the idea that the social vitality *of a group* can be destroyed through the physical or spiritual destruction of individual members of that group. Given that people of color and the working poor are targeted for arrest and incarceration, the prison system destroys the vitality of entire communities marked by race, class, and ethnicity. Despite the fact that Black scholars, activists and rappers have referred to the prison-industrial complex as a genocidal structure, white genocide scholars and the public have not heard them. Instead, public discussion is focused on the number of Black men in prison, rather than the routine tortures to which they are subject.

One of the rules of prison life in the United States is that the state does not provide prisoners with products for basic hygiene such as a toothbrush, toothpaste, shampoo, a brush, and so on. Prisoners must buy hygienic products through the commissary, and corporations make an enormous amount of money by selling their products in the prison at grossly inflated prices. At the state prison for women in Muncy, Pennsylvania each prisoner is given two pairs of underwear for an entire year (though they can purchase additional pairs at the commissary). Prisoners who do not have family members or friends contributing to their commissary accounts must rely on the salary they make in prison to buy hygienic products. The highest paid position receives twenty cents an hour. Further, most prisoners complain about the quality of the food and many prefer to skip meals altogether and eat the processed food they can buy from commissary. This leads to poor nutrition and poor health, and a disproportionate rate of cancer in the prisoner population. Prisoners do not have access to regular medical care. Further, prisoners can call their friends and family, but only at grossly inflated prices and, of course, under surveillance. Any infraction of prison rules may lead to cell restriction or solitary confinement; if the anguish caused by this isolation further prevents the prisoner from following the rules then she is put back into isolation. The only logic operating in these rules is the economy of social death, for they reinforce the powerlessness of populations marginalized and exploited for the sake of white supremacy.

Prisoners are subject to many genocidal practices that are interwoven into penal practices and state policies, though there is no *event* of genocide that is responsible for the predictable and preventable destruction of prisoners and their families. Genocide studies is based on the phenomenon of the *event* of genocide at the cost of analyzing the repetition of genocidal practices over time, made "normal" by the repetition of discursive practices that *normalize* them. A repetition of practices over time is a system, and a repetition that conceals a dysfunction is a pathology.[14] Instead of assuming the ontological basis of genocide as *Event*, we should instead consider genocide as a pathological pattern of sociopolitical practices. For our *sensibility* of genocide as Event supports our ability to interpret the excessive violence in our prisons as the tragic but inevitable consequence of any system of criminal punishment, rather than as the senseless, brutal infliction of torture against populations already marginalized by the racist and classist distribution of capital. However, as many underground rappers have illustrated in the lyrics to their songs, we cannot *see* the criminal justice system as structurally genocidal because we refuse to recognize the founding genocide of slavery that established the racial democracy in which we still live. The definition of genocide is not merely an academic matter but pertains to our ability to recognize and thus arrest the genocidal biopolitics that now informs the structure and conditions of incarceration.

Like the Nazi camps, the judicial system inside the prison is secret and autonomous; there is no federal oversight of the punitive decisions made by Department of Corrections (DOC) staff. This includes decisions to put prisoners in solitary confinement or deny them parole. For this reason, the DOC staff has absolute power over the prisoners. At the same time, prisoners are subject to an infinite number of mental and physical tortures that often erode their ability to resist their degradation. Our passive indifference to the extra-legal infliction of violence in our prisons is supported by our inability to see this violence as genocidal, as directed against racial and ethnic groups *as such* in order to traumatize them and undermine the vitality of their communities. A traumatic event is one that *could have and should have been prevented* and cannot be explained or justified with traditional narratives about the human condition or a democratic society. When a prisoner is killed by a correctional officer, that death does not count as either a murder or a sacrifice but as a "tragic" accident. The disarticulation of traumatic as tragic suffering serves to reinforce the indifference the public already exhibits toward the structural oppression of African Americans and in particular to the conditions of confinement which traumatize millions of Blacks on a daily basis and hover over all Black families as a daily existential threat, undermining their rights to life, liberty, and the pursuit of happiness.

In this sense, the term "genocide" is inherently political, as it designates a traumatic as opposed to a tragic form of suffering. The new Jim Crow is not a new phase of slavery, it is a continuation of genocidal practices that fail to be taken seriously in our political imaginary *as* genocidal. We need to expose the false basis of the distinction between American slavery and genocide if we are to expand our moral concern to the genocidal practices now inflicted on our prisoner population, who are legally confined, tortured, and exploited as slaves. If we define genocide as the infliction of social death, then the social death still inflicted on African Americans through the penal system indicates the repetition of genocidal violence in American history. As it is a system of genocide that is evil and illegal, we must abolish rather than reform our carceral archipelago. And in order to meet this critical moment in history, white genocide scholars have a particular responsibility to check the defensive refusal to examine the anti-Black presuppositions that have guided our distinctions and the use of our categories, our dominant lines of inquiry and our refusal to consider our work in relation to scholarship in critical race theory and testimonies by Black artists, scholars, activists and American prisoners who are always *out of sight* and *out of mind* to white genocide scholars even as they insist on the importance of their work for the sake of our moral compass.[15] Since the problem regards the white sensibility of anti-Black violence, it is also imperative to promote aesthetic works by Black artists that can affect the way we feel and imagine this violence. In this regard, I cannot do better than to recommend the new track JU$T by the group Run the Jewels, written in response to the American racial terror that preceded and followed the police murder of George Floyd: "The Thirteen Amendment says that slavery's abolished (shit) / Look at all these slave masters posing on your dollar (get it)."[16]

NOTES

1. Joy James, "Radicalizing Language and Law: Genocide, Discrimination, and Human Rights," in *Resisting State Violence: Radicalism, Gender, and Race in U.S.* (Minneapolis, MN: University of Minnesota Press, 1996), 54.
2. See Yehuda Bauer, *On the Holocaust and other Genocides*, Joseph and Rebecca Meyerhoff Annual Lecture, United States Holocaust Memorial Museum, October 5, 2006 (printed in Washington, DC: The Center for Advanced Holocaust Studies, 2007).
3. James, "Chapter 2: Radicalizing Language and Law," 46.
4. Bauer, *On the Holocaust and Other Genocides*, 18.
5. David Moshman, "Conceptual Constraints on Thinking about Genocide," *Journal of Genocide Research*, 3, (3), 431–50, p. 443.
6. Dirk Moses, "Conceptual Blockages and Definitional Dilemmas in the 'Racial Century': Genocides of Indigenous Peoples and the Holocaust," in *Colonialism and Genocide*, ed. D. Moses and D. Stone (New York, NY: Routledge, 2007), 148–80.
7. Bauer, *On the Holocaust and Other Genocides*, 18.
8. Götz Aly, *Hitler's Beneficiaries: Plunder, Racial War and the Nazi Welfare State* (New York, NY: Holt, 2005).
9. Timothy Snyder, *Black Earth: The Holocaust as History and Warning* (New York, NY: Tim Duggen Books, 2016).
10. Michelle Alexander, *The New Jim Crow: Mass Incarceration in an Age of Colorblindness* (New York, NY: The New Press, 2012).
11. Claudia Card, "Genocide is Social Death," in *Confronting Evil Terrorism, Torture, Genocide* (Cambridge MA: Cambridge University Press, 2010), 241–66.
12. Hannah Arendt, *The Origins of Totalitarianism* (New York, NY: Harcourt Brace, 1973), 444.
13. *We Charge Genocide: The Crime of Government Against the Negro People*, 3rd Edition, ed. William L. Patterson (New York, NY: International Publishers Co., 2017).
14. Alfred Frankowski, *The Post-Racial Limits of Memorialization: Toward a Political Sense of Mourning* (Lanham, MD: Lexington Books, 2015).
15. See especially, Norman R. Yetman, ed., *When I Was a Slave: Memoirs from the Slave Narrative Collection* (New York, NY: Dover, 2002); Patterson, *We Charge Genocide*; Alexander G. Weheliye, *Habeas Viscus: Racializing Assemblages, Biopolitics, and Black Feminist Theories of the Human* (Durham, NC: Duke University Press, 2014).
16. Run The Jewels, JU$T (featuring Pharrell Williams and Zack de la Rocha). RTJ4, Released: June 3, 2020.

Chapter 5

The "Post-Conflict State" in Africa

Challenging the Continued Normalization of Genocidal Violence

Patricia Daley

Between April 2015 and April 2016, the United Nations (UN) estimated that over 400 people were killed as a result of political violence in the "post-conflict" state of Burundi.[1] Other observers indicated that the figure may be around 1,155.[2] Mass graves were unearthed,[3] and what was perceived as a president seeking to hold on to power for an unconstitutional third term, despite considerable opposition, manifested into violence that some commentators have defined as "genocidal," as individuals and small groups have been targeted and massacred. Following the 2015 elections that returned the incumbent party and President Nkurunziza, critics of the state continued to be targeted; some 400,000 refugees fled the country; and, in the run-up to the 2020 elections, which Nkurunziza's chosen successor Evariste Ndayishimiye—his military adviser and former rebel—won, the UN Human Rights Commission documented gross violations including massacres and disappearances.[4] A question asked by observers is why the African Union (AU) or the UN have not intervened to stop the killings and what accounts for international indifference to the loss of black lives.

After the Rwandan genocide of 1994 when close to a million people were killed in twenty-one days, there were three prevailing views about how genocide in Africa could be averted in the future. First, African states in the 2002 constitutive acts of the AU pledged to intervene to prevent genocide and crimes against humanity, even if it meant bypassing sovereignty. Second, that application of reconciliation or transitional justice mechanisms would allow affected states to return to a level of peaceful co-existence. Truth and Reconciliation Commissions, modeled on the experience of post-apartheid South Africa, became the normative route through which societies were expected to heal themselves. Third, as the neoliberal era became embedded in political and economic thought, a prevailing view emerged among economists and was taken up by policy makers, that conflict in Africa can be attributed to the greed of the elite rather than grievances of the masses. This led to the promotion of power-sharing formulae, giving competing elites access to power through externally monitored elections linked to a market-oriented route to reconstruction whereby economic liberalization was expected to reduce elite capture of state resources and redistribute wealth. For *post-conflict* societies, this marked a shift from ideas that originated post–World War II that a developmental state was needed to rebuild a postwar society and ensure universal access to social welfare and economic development. There would be no Marshall Plan for post-conflict African societies. These assumptions together characterized what became known as the "liberal peace" and what formed a blueprint for post-conflict societies in Africa after the 1990s.[5] In the second decade of the twenty-first century, African lives continued to be lost at an intolerable rate as the structural and systemic conditions that led to wars in the first place remain unaddressed.

A critical question in the twenty-first century, therefore, is whether African lives matter to the international community. Since the period of European colonization, the Hobbesian maxim that life in Africa is necessarily "nasty, brutish, and short" has entered the popular consciousness.[6] Mass deaths of Africans caused by economic insecurity, natural disasters, famines, wars, and other crimes against humanity have become so normalized that the global community, including African leaders, have become inured to them. However, causes of premature death in Africa are primarily linked to the historical-structural conditions that underpin the modern state in Africa and its integration into the global political economy, and are mostly avoidable, given contemporary levels of global development. These conditions reproduce what I term "genocidal violence"—a violence rooted in colonial biopolitics of racialization and hierarchization of social identities for social and political control, in order to pursue extractive practices secured by state-sponsored violence aimed at eliminating competition and maintaining exclusivity of access.[7]

Despite the development of post–World War II international human rights regimes, Africa's political economy continues to be predicated on the devaluation of the lives of its people. Mutua has argued that international law is racialized, but this does not explain the lack of enforcement of human rights legislation by regional political unions.[8] This chapter argues that allowing practices that knowingly devalues the lives of other human beings to the point of destruction on the basis of their belonging to a social group constitutes genocide. Such practices have become embedded in modern African states, many of which have failed to transcend the racialized, ethnicized, and "scorched earth" policies that denied humanity to Africans and were used to legitimize colonial authority. Such practices are highly visible in traumatized, marginalized, and destitute post-conflict societies, and are aggravated when states see annihilation as the only response to political opposition. This leads us to ask: How can Africans overcome the coloniality of their existence and recalibrate the value of African lives on the continent and in the global political system?

In this chapter, I explore the conditions that have resulted in the genocidal violence in the twenty-first century by analyzing its manifestation in the liberal conceptualization of the "post-conflict" Burundian state. I examine the ideologies, practices, and relations that enable successive Burundi governments to eliminate members of their citizenry seeking greater representation and accountability and the barriers to external intervention, even when international and regional bodies demonstrate awareness of the gravity of the crimes against humanity. This chapter argues that the roots of Burundi's genocidal violence are embedded in a state that is unable to transcend its colonial heritage of racial hierarchical politics, exploitative economics, and institutions that dehumanize a substantial proportion of its citizens, hindering their participation in life sustaining activities. Consequently, militarized ethnic elites can deploy genocidal ideologies that justify the elimination of those perceived as threatening to their political and economic aspirations. In addition, Burundi is shown to be integrated into a regional and international coloniality in which African humanity is devalued, thus enabling global geopolitical interests to take precedence over saving African lives.

GENOCIDE AS NORMATIVE STATE PRACTICE IN AFRICA

It is only recently that the genocides of the European colonial powers in Africa have been given sufficient historical and scholarly analysis; such attention remains largely confined to the actions of the German colonial state in Namibia.[9] Other massacres of colonized people were represented as pacification or self-defense—the inevitable consequence of the wars to establish *Pax Europaea*. Such observations reflect the prevailing view that Africans were not *human enough* for their deaths to matter, or that such deaths were justified by the ends of the grander civilization mission.

Arising from the horror of the Jewish Holocaust in Western Europe, the Geneva Convention on Genocide of 1948 provides the basic principles by which violence is defined as genocide in international law. The Convention addresses acts that constitute the deliberate elimination of a *national, ethnical, racial or religious group* (Article II, *United Nations Convention on*

Genocide, 1948). Therefore, the ideology of genocide is built on the institutionalization of discrimination and violence as the path to homogeneity. We know that attempts to get the treatment of colonized Africans and Africans in the diaspora featured in the discussions that led to the drafting of the various post–World War II human rights legislations failed. For example, racial discrimination was not outlawed in the declaration establishing the UN Human Rights Commission, despite petition from African Americans.[10] Consequently, as Leonard argues, the United States represented itself at the time as inhabiting the moral high ground, while ensuring that it could continue to act amorally with respect to African Americans. Blocking attempts to include civil and economic rights and racial discrimination as human rights issues, the United States condemned its African American community to deprivation and marginalization for the long term.

In their colonies, Europeans' use of racialized and ethnicized ideologies in their rule of African societies ensured that discrimination became embedded in the modern state form that emerged in the late colonial and postcolonial period. On mainland Europe, scholars have linked modernity and the modern state form with genocide.[11] In Africa, scholars have started to address the historical, political, and economic conditions that have produced episodes of postcolonial genocide on the continent.[12] Central among the findings is the persistence into the postcolonial period of hierarchical thinking as the basis for the governance of a state via racially or ethnically exclusive lines.

Explanation as to why genocide occurs in some postcolonial African states and not in others have tended to use the narrow legalistic definition of genocide and to look for internal post-independence arguments. Straus, for example, focusing on political leadership, argues that the discourse of postcolonial leaders, the "founding fathers," can play a major role in dictating the sort of modern state that is imagined by the population.[13] However, while leaders sought to construct a homogenous nation-state modelled on European state ideals, visions of how a unified multiethnic society would work were rarely articulated and were often contentious. In a few contexts, visionary leaders who posed a threat to the colonial imagination of a postcolonial society were eliminated; the list includes Burundi's Prince Louis Rwagasore, who was assassinated in October 1961, just before independence.[14] While acknowledging that political leaders can set the tenor of the debate as to who belongs to the postcolonial political community, the historical memory of how the colonial state deals with difference is often reproduced in the bureaucratic and security practices of successive postcolonial regimes. Therefore, how the security apparatus reacts to protests, to political opposition, or those whose lives are seen as worthy of being saved directly or indirectly, and who are racially or ethnically superior to whom, remains significant.

It is within this context of the persistence of this racialized and ethnicized history that I seek to reconceptualize genocidal violence to encompass all manifestations of direct violence and structural violence: wars, massacres, child abduction, sexual violence, forced displacement, and disruption of livelihood activities that impact on the sustainability of the life of an individual or group that relates to membership in a group. Genocidal violence subjugates groups to a subhuman life, which at its extreme constitutes the elimination of individuals primarily because of their membership in that group. Genocidal violence is a process that can culminate in mass killings. It is important to understand how practices that are understood as genocidal can become embedded in state forms. Such practices arise from the normalization of genocidal ideologies that promote social hierarchies that devalue the humanity of particular social groups within the state. My contention is that the modern state, as it arose in many parts of Africa, with its racialized, ethnicized, and militarized tendencies now perpetuated through neoliberal capitalism, is genocidal and thus inimical to the prevention of genocidal violence.

The prevalence of conditions that produce genocide in Africa and the African diaspora and the growing awareness of the racialized nature of international human rights legislation point to the need to adopt different methodologies for understanding crimes that center on the destruction of groups of people or individuals belonging to certain groups. The Geneva Convention definition of genocide narrowly focuses on direct violence, excluding those characteristics that are fundamental to the economic and political systems in place. Hence, most analyses of genocide in Africa tend to focus on the relationship between perpetrators and victims preceding mass killings. The more populist interpretation focuses on primordial ethnic hatred as the rationale for violence, rather than violence being seen as the logical outcome of a state form and economic model built on exclusionary and discriminatory practices that result in the premature mass deaths of those in society who are deemed disposable.

A narrowly interpreted conventional definition also has implications for external intervention. The responsibility of the international community to act when genocide is occurring means that it is rarely called and often only called after meaningful or preventative intervention is too late to effectively save vast numbers of lives, as was the case in Rwanda. Two explanations for this reluctance are that targeting individuals, as opposed to mass killing, may not constitute genocide, and intervention would challenge state sovereignty. With regard to the first, death toll, what then should be the threshold for when genocide is declared in Africa? Reluctance to act undermines the fundamental principles of international human rights law, that those in power do not have the right to carry out crimes against humanity against their citizens within their state boundaries. However, the caveat is that in Africa, this principle, with few exceptions, has rarely been upheld.

To address this inaction, one must methodologically reframe how genocide is understood in Africa from populist essentialist ideas of ethnic hatred and the need for a strong state and, instead, situate manifestations of genocidal violence within a historical, structural, and geopolitical context, where the lives of some human beings are deemed less worthy of protection to the point that inaction against mass killings can be justified in the twenty-first century.[15] Even if ethnic identities are known to have been socially constructed during the colonial period, we need to understand how they have become potent forces that, as Ndlovu-Gatsheni finds in South Africa, "hang like a nightmare on the body politic . . . refusing to die, and continuing to throw up toxic questions around issues of . . . entitlement and ownership of resources."[16] Contemporary Burundi illustrates this argument well.

GENOCIDAL POLITICS IN "POST-CONFLICT" BURUNDI

The rush to declare a state *post-conflict*, as part of the liberal peace agenda, often obscures the failure to address the underlying conditions that triggered the period of conflict. In Burundi, before the 1990 civil war, genocidal politics were already rooted historically in the modern state form that took shape under colonial rule and over which there has been intense contestation in the postcolonial period. Elites of its main ethnic groups of Hutu and Tutsi have sought to resolve their political differences through massacres and unlawful killings of political opponents and their associates. Historians have shown that these ethnic identities, which reflected occupational differences in the precolonial period, were concretized under colonial rule through state promotion of racialized hierarchies that discriminated in favor of Tutsis—designated as being of Hamitic origin—and against Hutus and Twas—labeled as Bantu in origin. Using the military, in the post-independence period, the Tutsi were able to capture the state, with intra-Tutsi coups producing successive military regimes. The majority Hutu's quest for greater representation led to genocides in 1972, 1988, and in 1993 after the assassination of Melchior Ndadaye, the democratically elected Hutu president in October that year—six months after he had won the country's first multiparty elections since independence in 1962. Ndadaye's death was followed by a period of civil unrest, a Tutsi-dominated military coup, and a war from 1995 to the mid-2000s, continuing for almost six years after the 2000 Arusha Peace and Reconciliation Agreement was signed between the Tutsi-dominated military regime and the Hutu opposition parties. The Arusha Agreement thus sealed the interpretation of the conflicts as ethnic and made explicit the institutionalized ethnic differences that had prevailed since the colonial rule.

Burundi was labeled a *post-conflict state* after the 2005 democratic elections that saw the former rebel group party *Conseil National Pour la Défense de la Démocratie – Forces pour la Défense de la Démocratie* (National Council for the Defense of Democracy – Forces for the Defense of Democracy, or CNDD/FDD) gain power. The country's economic direction returned to the supervision of international financial institutions, and the UN and donors monitored the transition to peace along the guidelines provided by the Arusha Agreement. CNDD/FDD, the party that emerged victorious from the multiparty elections, was not a signatory of the Arusha Agreement after refusing to put down their weapons—a precondition for joining the peace negotiations. CNDD/FDD preferred to negotiate with the interim government that took control after Arusha, which it joined in 2003 as part of a power-sharing agreement.

For a brief period (2006–2015), Burundi was discussed as a success story by external observers, primarily because ethnicity, the main fault line along which groups were differentiated, had become mainstreamed with the institution of the Arusha-agreed ethnic (60/40 Hutu/Tutsi, respectively) and gender (30 percent women) quotas in the executive and legislative bodies of the state, and (50/50 Hutu/Tutsi) in the security services—the military and the police. For political parties to be registered, they had to abandon ethnic exclusivity and incorporate members of the four ethnic groups—Tutsi, Hutu, Ganwa, and Twa. However, since the main political parties, even during the Tutsi-dominated era were not ethnically exclusive, this was not too challenging except for those rebel groups turned political parties that were ideologically ethnically exclusive. Since ethnicity is only one of the fault lines in Burundi society (regional origins being quite strong), gaining representation from the other ethnic groups, if only marginally, would not have been impossible for political parties.

CNDD/FDD was viewed as the more moderate of the main Hutu-dominated rebel groups. Its Hutu leader Pierre Nkurunziza—an Evangelical Pentecostal Christian who reportedly believed that his presidency was ordained by God—appealed to the growing rural population that had been wooed mainly from Catholicism (the religion of the colonial power and elites), and promised redemption from Tutsi domination and greater access to the benefits of development, especially social welfare in the form of free schooling and maternal care. Cost-recovery fees, introduced as part of economic liberalization reforms, had caused considerable hardship in economically weak and war-torn Burundi; Nkurunziza was wise to make their eradication a central component of his election manifesto, thus separating himself from the establishment parties and his Hutu rebel rivals.

Elections that produced Nkurunziza's second term victory in 2010 were marred by pre-election violence and the withdrawal of the main opposition parties from the presidential elections. Hence, Nkurunziza was elected almost unopposed. His presidential term was characterized by militarized violence, with summary executions by the security services, especially the *Service National de Renseignements* (National Intelligence Service, or SNR); grenade attacks, and assassinations targeting opposition elements irrespective of ethnicity, increases in rape, theft, and murder by criminal elements, especially ex-paramilitary armed gangs, such by the *Imbonerakure*—the youth wing of the ruling party. This violence occurred despite the presence of a scaled-down UN peacekeeping mission[17] and the implementation of the UN-backed security sector reform program, or Disarmament Demobilization and Reintegration (DDR), which failed to fully disarm the rebels who were being demobilized. Liberal explanations view the persistence of militarism at the center of government as the result of a failure to transform "from rebel movement to political party."[18] Speight and Witting note the inability to separate the political wing from the military wing of the party, "underlining the importance of the core FDD military establishment for the maintenance of the regime."[19] However, the argument here is that militarism is foundational to the postcolonial state form and can only be excised through revolutionary practices.

Interpretation of the 2015 crisis in Burundi is often narrowed to the bid for a third presidential term by President Nkurunziza and viewed as the only element of the Arusha Agreement that was eroded.[20] The agreement states that the president should be appointed by popular vote for two terms; the 2005 Constitution states that the president should be elected by universal suffrage for a maximum of two terms. Nkurunziza claimed that his first tenure fell outside the terms of the agreement, as he was appointed president after his party won the elections. However, the government showed lack of commitment to other aspects of the agreement, exemplified by its tardiness in setting up the Truth and Reconciliation Commission and Special Tribunal, as recommended in the Arusha Agreement, and its gradual attempt to remove the agreed gender and ethnic quotas. In 2015, the law was changed to overturn the gender quota among the senior ministers in parliament, representing clear signs of a subscript that eluded international observers. Members of the former Tutsi elite, while respecting the ethnic split in government, grew increasingly alarmed by their marginalization from power by the CNDD/FDD government. Since Nkurunziza and CNDD/FDD were not party to the Arusha Agreement, it was perhaps too optimistic of observers to assume that they supported power sharing along ethnic lines.

The Nkurunziza government's reaction to those opposed to the third term, especially the violence it exacted, is reflective of the ways in which the genocidal state deals with demands for representation from marginalized groups. The destruction of the educated elite and those who are deemed potential competitors for state power, including members of the former Tutsi regime, is reminiscent of previous genocidal violence in Burundi. While the international community has been reluctant to use the label *genocide*, the targeting of Tutsi neighborhoods indicates that the state represents the opposition as ethnically motivated, despite clear evidence that those opposed to the third term come from all ethnic groups. For the Hutu-majority government, ethnicity has become an apparatus of the state—to be deployed to defend itself against any criticism or opposition. However, following the interpretation of genocide as outlined in this chapter, the term should extend to the killing of political opposition, irrespective of their ethnic affiliation.

This is not to say that ethnicity does not remain an important fault line in Burundi's society. The *de jure* institutionalization of ethnicity in the government of Burundi may have acted as a smokescreen, deluding those international policy makers pushing for peace. However, a nuanced examination of post-conflict Burundi reveals the saliency of an ethnic ideology and its intersection with a liberal peace and a geopolitical agenda that perpetuate a coloniality at the heart of which is the devaluation of African lives. The colonial origins of ethnicity are generally accepted by scholars as a source of conflict in Burundi.[21] The key issue is why it has persisted as a tool of mobilization by elites. An explanation is the continuing legacy of the differential incorporation of the ethnic groups into the state and the saliency of emotions of inferiority and superiority among people with limited opportunities for economic and social progress.

ECONOMIC INSECURITY: A CONDITION OF GENOCIDE

In this section, I focus on how, in the "post-conflict" era, the failure to transform the nature of Burundi's integration into the global economy has aggravated the intensity of the competition. Burundi's structural incorporation into the global political economy as a single-crop (coffee), export-oriented economy that is dependent on external aid for its social programs is the contemporary manifestation of what constitutes genocidal economics, which I described as "a form of economic engagement that require the physical elimination of competition. This type of economics comes from a form of competition for resources which is militarized, racialized and linked to the characterization of economic opponents as vermin."[22] It involves forced production, persistent insecurities, and impoverishment. Economists have argued that competition over access to resources explains the cycles of uprisings/

protests and repression that have plagued Burundian society.[23] There is no doubt that the state provides the main vehicle for capital accumulation in Burundi, in spite of attempts to widen access by neo-liberalizing and privatizing of the state's economic concerns, as part of the World Bank's supported Poverty Reduction and Growth Strategy programs.

The problem of framing the conflict in terms of economic insecurity is twofold. While an economically deterministic argument should be avoided for explaining genocide, economic insecurity can explain how elites perceive the threat from the political opposition and the violent measures they adopt to secure their tenure. Elite capture of the state is a consequence of Burundi's limited economic resources, high population density, land shortage, and heavy occupational dependency on small-holder agriculture for household income. Burundi's high level of aid dependency (more than 50 percent of government expenditure is derived from aid) means that resources channeled through the state remain critical to the accumulation of wealth. The economic situation in post-conflict Burundi improved only marginally in the 'post-conflict' period and has reached the crisis point after one year of political violence, dropping from the third poorest to the poorest country in the world in 2015, with a gross domestic product (GDP) of $315 USD, which declined further to $271 in 2018 and increased to $336 USD in 2019.[24] According to the African Development Bank, two-thirds of the population live below the poverty line and youth underemployment is 65 percent.[25] External aid is therefore integral to the maintenance of economic insecurity, and after aid from the European Union was suspended in 2015, the country's fiscal deficit rose.

The state has done little to address the need for improved livelihood opportunities among the predominantly rural population, where land pressures have intensified with repatriated refugees and the internally displaced seeking to regain control over lost agricultural land.[26] The resolution of land conflicts has been subject to political interference and discrimination in favor of those with political contacts. Lack of opportunities for livelihood reconstruction continues to ensure that the masses of Burundians are vulnerable to premature death. Even though President Nkurunziza's declaration of free schooling and hospital care was welcomed by the masses, it was not accompanied by additional resources to deal with the increased demand. Hence, the post-conflict period has seen public sector strikes and even the return of former refugees to their countries of asylum.[27]

Another important socioeconomic legacy of colonial, racial, and ethnic discrimination in Burundi is the persistence of inequality in access to education and social progress. The colonial and postcolonial states' exclusion of Hutus and Twas from higher education meant that only a small fraction of Hutus was educated, and this was mainly through seminaries in the Congo. Consequently, generations of highly educated Tutsis benefited from postcolonial regimes that facilitated their access to public sector employment. Their educational advantage enabled their recruitment by multinational and international non-governmental organizations in Burundi and has contributed to their grievance with respect to their marginalization from the public sector by the current regime. Resentment of this historic entitlement underlies some of the government's criticism of civil society, especially those led by Tutsi activists.

GENOCIDE AND IMPUNITY

The extent to which a society that has been exposed to episodes of genocide can attain peace without addressing impunity is questionable. In contemporary Burundi, the fact that those who have committed atrocities have not been brought to justice only works to further entrench the present state relations with older ethnic resentments. The issue for the facilitators of the Arusha peace process was that the majority of the participants in the negotiations were implicated in crimes against humanity; in order to prevent further bloodshed, the facilitators agreed that the promise of immunity was a precondition for negotiation and a peaceful Burundi. Apart from those who were involved in the assassination of the democratically elected president, a law of immunity was passed in August 2003 covering crimes with a political aim committed after 1 July 1962 to the date of promulgation (27 August 2003). This was done to protect those who had been sentenced (in absentia) for atrocities, including Pierre Nkurunziza, and to enable full participation of all the protagonists in the power-sharing government and multiparty elections. In addition, the CNDD/FDD government has demonstrated an unwillingness to tackle impunity. In 2006, it passed two laws giving amnesty to a total of 1453 political prisoners, whose release from jail was challenged by human rights organizations.[28]

Furthermore, the CNDD/FDD government embarked on protracted consultations and negotiations, thus delaying the establishment of the Truth and Reconciliation Commission that would allow prosecution of those who commit atrocities. The National Assembly passed a law as early as September 1, 2004, allowing the UN to set up a non-Judicial Truth Commission, with a substantial international component and the creation of a special chamber within the Burundi justice system to address crimes against humanity. To date, however, the terms of the Commission and the Special Tribunal are still being negotiated; the international component has been reduced and civil society and human rights groups that participated in the consultations have not been invited to sit on the commission.[29] Such an approach reinforces the pervasive culture of impunity and makes the April 2016 announcement that the International Criminal Court (ICC) would investigate whether to bring charges of crimes against humanity against Burundian perpetrators of the recent violence a welcome development in the pursuit of justice.[30] It is doubtful whether the ICC will find the political environment in Burundi and the region conducive to investigate and pursue cases.

For political expediency, policy makers have sought to promote political stability rather than transitional justice in Burundi.[31] Observers assume that genocide was the outcome of competitive, embedded ethnic divisions and could be prevented by first focusing on power sharing. Burundi's transition to electoral democracy occurred during a period when power sharing, rather than the winner-takes-all model of reconciling political differences, became normalized in international peace and reconciliation agreements. The South African example, in which those who committed crimes against humanity were not punished, reinforced the idea that African lives did not matter. While the South African Peace and Reconciliation Agreement may have prevented further warfare in a context in which the minority held the reins of power, especially the security forces, the elites among the minority had come to the realization that their racialized domination was no longer sustainable in a globalized marketplace and a post–Cold War context. A gradual integration of minority elites in a genocidal system allowed them to maintain their economic hegemony in the new South Africa. In the Burundi case, the Tutsi-minority elite, conscious that majoritarian electoral democracy would remove them from power, agreed to first share, then relinquish power because their economy was dependent on development aid that would have been further curtailed if the government had remained intransigent. Multiethnic political parties and power sharing allowed them to maintain limited access to power within the new dispensation.

However, the ethnic dimension of state-sponsored violence is clearly linked to who controls the security services. Central to the security of the minority Tutsi was their domination of the security services, especially the military and the intelligence services. This was seen as essential to their ethnic group security in light of genocides against Rwandan Tutsis in 1959 and 1994. Consequently, for the majority of its postcolonial history, Burundi was ruled by Tutsi-dominated military regimes with intra-Tutsi regional and class rivalries producing coups in 1966, 1976, 1987, and 1996. The disproportionate 50 percent Tutsi representation in the new integrated security services, as agreed at Arusha, arose from Tutsi security concerns and was a guarantee of their safety. As integration started in the lower ranks, most of the senior ranks were Tutsi up until recently. It is with this background that the May 2015 attempted coup and the assassinations of former military officers should be analyzed. Three of the coup leaders, a general and two police commissioners, were arrested and charged with attempting to overthrow the state. The principal leader, a general and former chief of intelligence, evaded capture. Government purges against potential Hutu and Tutsi threats forced many senior officials to flee the country, including the then-deputy vice-president of the National Assembly.

An important question relates to the commitment of those groups who were outside the Arusha process to its recommendations. Because of their ethnic ideology and their refusal to put down arms, the Hutu rebel groups did not participate in the Arusha negotiations. Consequently, while they finally agreed to power sharing in parliament and integration into the armed forces post-Arusha, the extent of their willingness to work with the Tutsi has not been proven. No doubt, some individuals saw power sharing as an opportunity for self-enrichment, but also to settle scores with Tutsi extremists. If President Nkurunziza saw himself as a messiah figure, this was a consequence of the Hutu people's long quest to regain their humanity and justice in Burundi.

Modern Burundi's histories of genocide remain etched into the memory of the people. With cycles of mass killings that have a predominantly ethnic character, ethnic ideology remains a mobilizing force among some sectors of the Hutu and Tutsi populations. Straus argues that genocide occurs when the "target population is viewed as inherently dangerous with interests that are inimical to those of the predator . . . and the perpetrators experience themselves as vulnerable to the threat from the target group."[32] Many children of the 1972, 1988, and 1990s massacres, in which Hutus were the main targets, are now in power. Hutu ministers and government advisors were survivors of massacres dating back to the 1970s; for example, the foreign minister Alain Nyamitwe lost his father and three uncles during the 1972 genocide and two cousins in 1991 and 1994. He, along with President Ndayishimiye, narrowly escaped genocide in 1994—an experience that Nyamitwe has documented.[33] However, equally persistent are regimes that obscure and conceal this history on the one hand and promote the normalization of violence on the other. This means that understanding genocidal violence means thinking through its cyclical character; it means thinking through its moments of mass violent activity, and the moments of peaceful repose.

Rethinking genocide in Burundi means looking beyond ethnicity to consider how the state deals with members of the opposition who have never been solely from one ethnic group. Opposition to the CNDD/FDD leadership and to the president's third term came from a variety of sources—from within his own party, from other Hutu-dominated parties, and from social organizations. A defining feature of how the state reacts to oppositional voices with an ethnic script is exemplified by the state security services' targeting of predominantly Tutsi areas of the capital Bujumbura in their search for critics—termed "terrorists." Multiethnic human rights groups in Burundi calling for the president to respect the term limits are represented as threats to Burundi's democracy and development—some implying that they are Tutsi seeking a return to a Tutsi-dominated regime. Although an ethnic tally has not been taken of the dead, anecdotal evidence suggests that those killed are predominantly from the Tutsi ethnic group.

Suspicions of a regional Tutsi/Hamitic conspiracy have long pervaded the politics of Burundi and neighboring Rwanda, Uganda, and the Democratic Republic of Congo and can be revived by unscrupulous politicians in order to justify their unconstitutional and violent hold on power. It is the regional dimension of the ethnic ideology that has partly shaped the geopolitical reaction to Burundi's 2015 crisis.

MILITARIZED PEACE (STABILIZATION) AND POST–COLD WAR GEOPOLITICS

In addition to ethnic and demographic deterministic interpretations of the Burundi conflict, there are realist interpretations of the politics behind nonintervention by the international community. Realist interpretations tend to argue that the inadequate international response to Burundi's political turmoil has to do with the country's lack of strategic economic resources, proposing that countries with the capacity to intervene to prevent acts of genocide will not do so if their strategic interests are not threatened. International inaction to the reports of earlier genocides in Burundi and that of Rwanda in 1994 could be linked to the absence of any immediate threat to strategic resources; however, we should also not underestimate the extent to which the legacy of colonial racism and eugenics continue to structure a global system in which racialized assumptions about the value of African lives to an international human rights regime are considered to be worth less than, for example, American lives.[34]

A narrow focus on the political entity of Burundi can miss the bigger picture—especially the significance of Burundi's geopolitical position, adjacent to mineral-rich areas of the eastern Democratic Republic of Congo, and more recently, the country's contribution to imperial wars, in the form of regional and international peacekeeping forces. One could argue that tolerance of genocidal violence, since 2015, persists because of the contemporary strategic importance of the country, especially its contribution to the West's global war on terror. Furthermore, in the twenty-first century, genocidal violence persists because of the way in which post-conflict Burundi has been integrated into militarized global geopolitics. For Burundians, the *liberal peace* comprises not just an externally derived framework, but also the country's participation in globalized peacekeeping that seeks to integrate armies from the global South in peacekeeping missions in other areas of the global South.

Such moves arose from the reluctance of the United States to commit significant numbers of troops to peacekeeping in Africa after the 1992 debacle in Somalia when American troops were killed.

International peacekeeping has been promoted as a mechanism to earn foreign exchange for African armies and governments, as a solution to the integration of rebel armies into post-conflict forces, and as a means of providing military assistance from Western governments without Western domestic public outcry with respect to military aid.[35] Soon after the integration of its security forces with those of the former rebels, Burundian security personnel were trained to participate in the African Union Mission in Somalia (AMISOM), providing the second-largest contingency.[36] Supposedly, as part of the DDR and in support of its peacekeeping mission, the entire Burundi National Defense Force was trained by the US military and private military contractors (Northrop Grumman) under the US government's Africa Contingency Operations Training and Assistance (ACOTA) program.[37] Furthermore, Burundi obtained drones from the United States as part of a military aid package, which according to the BBC, includes "body armor, night-vision gear, communications, and surveillance systems" for "counter-terrorism" activities "to support Burundi's AMISOM role."[38] Additional support and training have been provided to the Burundi police by Belgium and Canada as part of the Security Sector Reform program. In 2012, Stockholm International Peace Research Institute (SIPRI) estimated that Burundi had the highest military expenditure (2.39 percent of the gross domestic product) in the East African community.[39] Consequently, a CNDD/FDD government with a trained security force equipped with military hardware for peacekeeping is in a strong position to withstand political opposition and potential rebel incursion.

Despite a wealth of criticisms of the liberal peace, especially its externally derived solutions and its failure at disarmament, policy makers persisted, eventually calling the prevailing condition "stabilization" rather than peace.[40] Through the process of stabilization, war ceased, but extreme violence persisted.

WHY REGIONAL NON-INTERVENTION?

Clearly, regional political bodies or human rights organizations in Africa lack the political will to intervene to prevent crimes against humanity. The AU's predecessor, the Organization of African Unity, was also criticized for its inaction to prevent the 1994 Rwandan genocide. If the more proactive clause in the Constitutive Act of the AU was to prevent further non-interventions, it failed in 2015 Burundi. The declaration by the AU's Peace and Security Council to send a prevention and protection force was rejected by the Burundi government, which stated that it would treat the move as an act of aggression; the AU backed down.[41] One explanation for the AU's retreat relates to the lack of commitment by African leaders to overthrow a president seeking a third term when only a minority among them have respected constitutional third-term limits or, institutionally, to a lack of agreement between the AU's various policy organs.[42] While it seems plausible to leave the resolution of the political crisis in Burundi to the East African Community (EAC), of which Burundi is a member, the selection of its long-serving president, Yoweri Museveni, as the mediator meant that the Burundian opposition could not have any confidence in a regionally mediated resolution that would go against the third term.

Another explanation for the AU's stance is the assertion of sovereignty by the state of Burundi, which has threatened to attack any force that violates its territory. It is in this context that, even with reports of summary executions by the security services and the uncovering of mass graves, the AU reneged on its promise to send a peacekeeping force. Making sovereignty sacrosanct over the lives of citizens subjected to extreme violence undermines the very values that the AU in its Constitution seeks to uphold. One could also argue that the AU, often described as a club of African leaders, could not summon the moral authority necessary to intervene—thus reinforcing the view that African lives can be violated with impunity.

Within the Great Lakes region of Africa, the Burundi government draws on preexisting ethnic animosities to support the regime's defiant stance. The regime has adopted a strategy of accusing the Tutsi-dominated neighboring state of Rwanda of fomenting strife and instability in Burundi, implying that opposition to the third term did not arise from grievances within the country. When President Kagame of Rwanda issued a warning about genocide in Burundi,[43] in reprisal, Burundi promoted the view that Burundians in Rwandan refugee camps were being trained by Rwanda to attack Burundi (evidence of which remains weak).[44] What is certain is that the 2015 crisis appeared to have ended the cordial relations that existed between the Burundian and Rwandan governments.

Burundi's participation in the reinvigorated neoliberal-oriented EAC is seen as critical to the balance of power within the organization (siding with Tanzania against Rwanda, Uganda, and Kenya) and the opening up of the markets through the movement of goods and resources across states. President Nkurunziza was perceived as the sole person who can provide the stability for markets to function. Such a perspective has been adopted by regional leaders, in spite of Nkurunziza's violations of his citizens' human rights, but it is also representative of a continuation of the "strong man as leader" approach that produced and sustained Cold War dictatorial regimes in Africa prior to the move toward multi-partyism in the 1990s.

Attempts at mediation by the EAC appear to be a replication of the regional mediation that preceded the Arusha Agreement of 2000. The CNDD/FDD government's refusal to negotiate with opposition forces that have used violence echoed the position adopted by the Tutsi-dominated government of Burundi in the 1990s. Even if coup leaders were to join the negotiations, the outcome is not likely to be the radical transformation of politics in Burundi that is needed to end genocidal violence, as it would be difficult to identify those around the table who are not implicated in genocide.

CONCLUSIONS

If genocide is one of the most heinous crimes of our times—a crime against humanity—then we should look to reveal and challenge its manifestations, whenever and wherever they occur. At the core of genocidal thinking is an ideology that some human lives are worth more than others. Genocidal ideologies pervaded the last two centuries, as the political and economic structures that have been emplaced are inherently discriminatory and unequal—privileging certain people and places over others.

The contemporary position of black lives in post-conflict Burundi arose out a particular historical context; that is, the structural conditions by which African states have been integrated into the global geopolitical economy, from the colonial period to the present, which were predicated on the devaluation of the lives of the African masses. This genocidal economics was justified during the colonial period by the racialization and ethnicization of African societies, which ensured differential access to power and impoverishment for the excluded—a condition that postcolonial elites sought to perpetuate. In such contexts, the violent conditions in which people live their everyday lives is genocidal, even when it does not result in outright wars or massacres of the *other*.

Decades of state-sponsored discriminatory practices in Burundi are unlikely to be transformed by the re-imposition of the same material and political conditions that prevailed prewar, even if the spoils are now divided between power-sharing ethnic elites. The modalities of the *liberal peace* have only reinforced those extreme conditions rather than mitigate them. In "post-conflict" Burundi, the conditions of war and peace have merged and are almost indistinguishable. In addition, the terms "peace" and "security" have become problematic when the contemporary Burundi state can claim, through UN peacekeeping, to be contributing to global peace, yet respond with hostility to attempts to promote peace internally. Little Burundi is mimicking the rhetoric and actions of global superpowers whose global moral high ground is not reflected locally in their treatment of migrants and nonwhite citizens.

In essence, genocidal ideologies in Burundi persist because the successive Burundian governments and the international community have not demonstrated that Burundian lives matter or have sought to build an anti-colonial unified nation, as envisioned by Prince Rwagasore at the dawn of independence—a fact that all Burundians seem to accept. Burundians have been offered political stability over justice and the ending of genocidal practices. A culture of impunity results in persistent fears of economic marginalization and physical elimination of the opposition, especially among Burundi's militarized ethnic elites. If leadership is critical to whether massacres take place, how can one ensure that those who espouse a nonviolent vision of Burundi come to the fore?

Rethinking genocide in Burundi means considering how the lives of the Burundian people have become so devalued that they can be eliminated without intervention. It is only through an understanding of the complexity of this history and its continued manifestations that the first steps for imagining another Burundi can occur.

NOTES

1. "Senior UN Official Warns Burundi's Tensions Could Fuel Violence throughout Great Lakes Region," United Nations News Centre, March 22, 2016, http://www.un.org/apps/news/story.asp?NewsID=53522#.VzNPCllcC8A.

2. "Armed Conflict Location and Event Datasets," *Country Report: Burundi Crisis Year One*, May, 2016, http://www.acleddata.com/wp-content/uploads/2016/05/ACLED-Country-Report-Burundi-May-2016.pdf.

3. "Burundi: Satellite Evidence Supports Witness Accounts of Mass Graves of 11 December Violence," *Amnesty International*, January 29, 2016, index number: AFR 16/3337/2016, http:www.amnestyinternational/en/documents/afr16/3337/2016/en/.

4. UN Council for Human Rights, *Rapport final détaillé de la Commission d'enquête sur le Burundi*, September 13, 2019, A/HRC/42/CRP.2.

5. Mark Duffield, *Global Governance and the New Wars: The Merging of Development and Security* (London: Zed Books, 2001).

6. See Thomas Hobbes, *Leviathan: With Variant Selections from the Latin Edition of 1688*, ed. E. Curely (Indianapolis, IN: Hackett Publishing Co., 1994).

7. Patricia Daley, *Gender and Genocide in Burundi: The Search for Spaces of Peace in Central Africa* (Bloomington, IN: Indiana University Press, 2008).

8. Makau Mutua, "Savages, Victims and Saviours: The Metaphor of Human Rights," *International Law Journal*, 42, (1), 2001, 201–45.

9. Bibi Khatija Khan, "The Kaiser's Holocaust: The Coloniality of German's Forgotten Genocide of the Nama and the Herero of Namibia," *African Identities*, 10, (3), 2012, 211–20.

10. See Carole Elaine Leonard, *Eyes Off the Prize: The United Nations and the African American Struggle for Human Rights, 1944–1955* (Cambridge, MA: Cambridge University Press, 2003).

11. Zygmunt Bauman, *Modernity and the Holocaust* (Malden, MA: Polity Press, 1989).

12. Mahmood Mamdani, *When Victims Become Killers: Colonialism, Nativism, and the Genocide in Rwanda* (Princeton, NJ: Princeton University Press, 2001); and Daley, *Gender and Genocide in Burundi*.

13. Scott Straus, *Making and Unmaking Nations: War, Leadership, and Genocide in Modern Africa* (Ithaca, NY: Cornell University Press, 2015).
Click here to enter text.

14. Jules Chomé, "L'Affaire Rwagasore," *Remarques Congolaises: Hebdomadaire Pan Africain d'Information et de Documentation*, December 14, 1962, Bruxelles.

15. Karina Jaworski, "The Methodological Crisis of Theorising Genocide in Africa: Thinking with Agamben and Butler," *African Identities*, 10, (3), 2012, 349–65.

16. Sabelo J. Ndlovu-Gatsheni, "Racialized Ethnicities and Ethnicized Races: Reflections on the Making of South Africanism," *African Identities*, 10, (4), 2012, 407–22, p. 407.

17. Burundi had peacekeeping missions from 2003–2006—first the African Union Peace-keeping Mission (AMIB) which was taken over in 2004 by the United Nations (ONUB), which was scaled down at the request of the Burundi government, despite clear evidence of continued violations of human rights.

18. Gervais Rufyikiri, "The Post-wartime Trajectory of CNDD-FDD Party in Burundi: A Facade Transformation of Rebel Movement to Political Party," *Civil Wars*, 19, (2), 2017, 220–48.

19. Jeremy Speight and Katrin Wittig, "Pathways from Rebellion: Rebel-Party Configurations in Cote d'Ivoire and Burundi," *African Affairs*, 117, (466), 2017, 21–43, p. 41.

20. Barack Obama, "Remarks by President Obama to the People of Africa," *The White House*, July 28, 2015, https://www.whitehouse.gov/the-press-office/2015/07/28/remarks-president-obama-people-africa.

21. See Mamdani, *When Victims Become Killers*; Daley, *Gender and Genocide in Burundi*.

22. Daley, *Gender and Genocide in Burundi*, 15.

23. Floribert Ngaruko and D. Nkurunziza Janvier, "An Economic Interpretation of Conflict in Burundi," *Journal of African Economies*, 9, (3), 2000, 370–409.

24. "Burundi's Economy Battered by the Crisis," *The Citizen*, May 2, 2016, http: Tradingeconomics.com.

25. Africa Development Bank, *Burundi Economic Outlook*, 2020, https://www.afdb.org/en/countries/east-africa/burundi/burundi-economic-outlook.

26. Jillian Keenan, "The Blood Cries Out," *Foreign Policy*, March 27, 2015, http://foreignpolicy.com/2015/03/27/the-blood-cries-out-burundi-land-conflict/; Rosine Tchatchoua-Djomoa, Gemma van der Haar, Han van Dijka, and Mathijs van Leeuwen,

"Intricate Links: Displacement, Ethno-Political Conflict, and Claim-Making to Land in Burundi," *Geoforum*, February 2020, 143–51.

27. Andrea Purdekova, "Barahunga Amahoro—They Are Fleeing Peace!' The Politics of Re-Displacement and Entrenchment in Post-War Burundi," *Journal of Refugee Studies*, 30, (1), 2016, 1–25.

28. Stef Vandeginste, *Stones Left Unturned: Law and Transitional Justice in Burundi* (Cambridge, UK: Intersentia, 2010).

29. Stef Vandeginste, "Burundi's Truth and Reconciliation Commission: How to Shed Light on the Past While Standing in the Dark Shadow of Politics?" *The International Journal of Transitional Justice*, 6, (2), 2012, 1–11.

30. Thomas Escritt, "ICC to Investigate Past Year's Deadly Violence in Burundi," *Reuters*, April 27, 2016, http://www.reuters.com/article/us-warcrimes-burundi.

31. Vandeginste, *Stones Left Unturned*.

32. Straus, *Making and Unmaking Nations*, 33.

33. Nyamitwe, *J'ai échappé au massacre de l'université*.

34. See Mutua, "Savages, Victims and Saviours"; and Jemina Pierre, "Race in Africa Today: A Commentary," *Cultural Anthropology*, 28, (3), 2012, 547–51.

35. Elizabeth Dickinson, "For Tiny Burundi, Big Returns in Sending Peacekeepers to Somalia," *Christian Science Monitor*, December 22, 2011, http://www.csmonitor.com/World/Africa/2011/1222/For-tiny-Burundi-big-returns-in-sending-peacekeepers-to-Somalia.

36. International Crisis Group, *Burundi: The Army in Crisis. Crisis Group Africa Report N 247*, April 5, 2017.

37. Ibid.

38. "Uganda and Burundi to get US Drones to Fight Islamists," *British Broadcasting Corporation (BBC) News*, June 28, 2011, http://www.bbc.co.uk/news/world-africa-13946702.

39. "Uganda, Burundi lead East Africa in Military Spending," *The East African*, April 16, 2014, http://www.theeastafrican.co.ke/news/Uganda--Burundi-lead-East-Africa-in-military-spending.

40. Jan Bachmann and Gelot Linnéa, "Between Protection and Stabilization? Addressing the Tensions in Contemporary Western Interventions in Africa: An Introduction," *African Security*, 5, (3–4), 2012, 129–41.

41. Milton Nkosi, "Has the African Union Let Down Burundi?" *British Broadcasting Corporation (BBC)*, February 1, 2016, http://www.bbc.com/news/world-africa-35462079.

42. Kasaija Phillip Apuuli, "The 'Speculated' Intervention of the East African Standby Force (EASF) in the Sudan: Lessons from its Failed Deployment in Burundi," *African Security Review*, 28, (3–4), 2019, 229–44.

43. "Rwandan President Kagame Warns of Escalating Violence in Burundi," *Reuters*, November 8, 2015, http://www.reuters.com/article/us-burundi-politics-rwanda.

44. "Burundi and DRC Implore UN to Take Action Against Rwanda," *African News*, http://www.africanews.com/2016/02/19/burundi-and-drc-implore-un-to-take-action-against-rwanda/.

Chapter 6

Hermeneutical Aesthetics, Commemoration, and Mourning in Post-Genocide Rwanda

Alfred Frankowski

In 2019, Rwandan president Paul Kagame ushered in the twenty-fifth commemoration of the Rwandan Genocide against the Tutsi by stating that "Genocide hibernates as denial. Revisionism is not merely demeaning, but profoundly dangerous. . . . We exist in a permanent state of commemoration."[1] His statement captures how commemoration carries with it a responsibility of the present community to remember the history of genocide for the propriety of future generations. It also acknowledges how complicated the relationship is between genocide and commemoration since no genocide appears in the clear and distinct sight of reason, but rather hides in the thickets and weeds of present forms of denial and evasion.

It is the relation of the *danger* and the meaning of a *permanent state of commemoration* that concerns this chapter. It is unquestionable that the Rwandan genocide against the Tutsi remains part of the global discourse on genocide or that its commemoration practices stand out as models for genocide remembrance. How and what is remembered remains a question that resides within the fact that Rwanda is one of the rare cases where a genocide occurs on the African continent and it is not reduced to a conflict, ignored as a natural course of events, or simply denied outright. Genocide in Africa and against the globally black is generally political violence without sense or context. The danger of not remembering is also the danger of remembering that which has been seen as illegitimate. To be in a permanent state of commemoration means to always be tethered to the past but it also means that commemoration is actively in play in the present as a social and political force.

Throughout this chapter, I will focus on the philosophical questions that arise from Rwandan forms of commemoration. In the first section of this chapter, and in agreement with contemporary genocide scholars, I will argue that commemoration of genocide is both necessary for genocide research and historically linked to denied political violence of colonialism. Unlike most genocide scholars, my approach to commemoration aesthetics, however, follows in the tradition of hermeneutical aesthetics. Hermeneutical aesthetics was developed by Hans-Georg Gadamer and was often also associated with both phenomenology and critical theory.[2] In both phenomenology and critical theory, the intersections between art and world raise questions about the normativity of the social world and the meaning of the artworks and the people who connect with them. Hermeneutics has also been developed in African philosophy by philosophers like Tsenay Serequeberhan and Okonda Okolo, the historian Achille Mbembe, and critical theorists to problematize and invite further questioning of how we normalize the displacement of and violence directed toward Africa.[3] In all of these approaches, the world and its experiential, social, historical meaning is called into question in its normativity. Hermeneutics requires a critical understanding of interpretation. I use this approach to question where the sensible diverges or contradicts the discursive, and where remembrance of the genocide necessitates a forgetting of the context of the genocide altogether. By examining the differences between sites of massacre and National Mourning, I will lay out the questions that emerge in the intersections between the political and aesthetic meanings of commemoration. Furthermore, I inquire into their meaning in a post-genocide context and raise a question about the political horizon in which post-genocide aesthetics continues to develop. I will focus on how this provides a critical reading of commemoration, but also challenges us to engage the question of what genocidal violence means in present, and how this is intertwined with histories of colonialism, on the one hand, and a political sense of a post-genocide Rwanda as a global political entity, on the other.

We repay the debt of those deaths poorly if we forget or repeat the past. We repay them equally poorly if we never learn to think their violence within our own world, and as part of our own questioning. My questions concerning memory are questions concerning both the limits of coming to terms with the past and the inability to interpret present violence as anything more than history. How do we see violence as violence?

GENOCIDE DISCOURSE, COMMEMORATION, AND THE CONTEXT OF COLONIALISM

Genocide scholars have added a wealth of conceptual tools and analyses to the literature on commemoration. They have developed critical approaches to understanding the politics of memory, the importance of histories that are remembered or forgotten, and further questioned the uses and abuses of museums and public memorials. What is clear across of all of this is that the role of memory and genocide is fraught with questions of whose story is legible, what narratives are permitted, and, of course, what is silenced, lost, denied. What is less clear is how the violence of genocide is mediated by the commemoration discourse itself. When considering the dearth of analyses of genocide against people of Africa and the diaspora, on the one hand, and problems that arise in terms of memory in the context of histories of colonialism, on the other, these questions are amplified to a greater extent. The interpretive problems of commemoration are more than discursive challenges and they raise critical questions for hermeneutical aesthetics about the limits of interpretation and the limits of the sensible, especially in terms of genocide commemoration in specifically African contexts.

The problem that genocide commemoration poses is as geopolitical as it is historical. Genocide in Africa, against Africans, rarely raises critical questions about how we understand, analyze, and shape the discourse on genocide more generally. In part this is due to the colonial worldview that has normalized the forms of political violence and divestment toward the colonized. Dirk Moses argues,

> The phobic consciousness responsible for this genocide continues to baffle historians because, in the main, they have confined their search to European sources. The recent interest in colonial genocides, stimulated in part by the rediscovery of Hannah Arendt's writings on imperialism, goes some way in situating the Nazi project in global patterns.[4]

As Moses points out, the problem is not just that colonialism has failed to be factored into historian accounts of colonized spaces, but that a Eurocentric worldview shapes the way we interpret this colonialism. In fact, the telling of history does little more than to set out the past violence within the discursive limits of a memory that fails to confront its political history as violence.

The issues of the sensible are not simply about what we know or do not know, or what we accept and what we deny, but rather how they facilitate and open or block modes of interpretation and methods of further address, and concern what it means to live a particular situation, and are obscured within historical approaches that are insufficiently clear about the discursive challenges that are embedded in a history without reference to the violence of colonialism. Following Moses analysis of the problem of colonialism, the global shift he argues for recognizes a contradiction between historians who situate genocide only in European contexts without problematizing the global/colonial context in which these genocides came to be. But Moses also argues that the political history of genocide cannot be accounted for without theorizing this political violence within the contexts created out of colonialism, on the one hand, and without understanding this context as epistemically a dynamically political and cultural process, on the other.[5] Moses concludes that, for the colonized, a non-consoling history is importantly part of the process of recovering a politics after trauma. His position argues for a radical reframing of commemoration aesthetics. While his approach distinctly creates the space for new narratives to be heard and challenge the norms of discourse, he does not further analyze how commemoration embeds modes of silence itself.[6] The problem is not just about what we know, but how we know what we know, but the context of knowing and knowing at the level of the sensible and what is produced as sensible within the history of colonialism.

Keeping colonialism in mind as context presents a second set of interpretative challenges for commemoration aesthetics of genocide. Colonialism must be part of the framework, but it also cannot collapse the singularity of its effects on specific countries and contexts and without this, there is no real understanding that could result. In *Rwanda's Genocide,* Kingsley Chiedu Moghalu argues that the genocide cannot be understood as anything other than the expansion of European colonial rule, an expansion that continued practices of destabilization that bore direct relation to their articulation as being concrete in the elimination of one another.[7] This expansion in some cases meant a change of governing, in others, slavery, and still in others, genocide. What is lost in this framework is that colonialism shifts from a politics between sovereigns to sovereignty as violence. For this reason, Alexander Hinton argues that "to understand the relationship between genocide and colonialism, we must be attuned to more than the colonial encounter as described by the colonizers: we need to examine the dynamism of the encounter on the local level, as cultural knowledge was transformed . . . and the historical legacy was transformed in the postcolonial period."[8] Hinton argues for just this specific examination of the relations that are inscribed in colonialism, both social and lived, political and historical. He further argues that the pattern of colonial animosity that shaped and divided the society into civilized and savage at the cultural level continues to inform the subjects of genocidal violence.[9]

It is clear that Hinton's critique retains the need for focus on relations that continue and abide, that are dynamic and shift within the context of colonialism. However, these also present interpretive challenges in that the narratives of the colonized are not so clear. We need to be attentive to how the shift between colonized histories, knowledges, and discourses are themselves silent or complicit in distancing, reframing, and denying modes of violence as part of the history and as violence. This occurs especially when violence is thought only in terms of history, or histories denied, and not as laying claim to the interpretive frameworks employed in the critical inquiry and discourse itself. Being attentive to the role of interpretation at the level of the sensible so that contradictions between the discursive and sensible can be confronted is not simply part of what it means to be analytically or conceptually clear; it is entailed in confronting political violence as violence despite the ways we are culturally trained to minimize or distort this context.

By framing the issue of commemoration within hermeneutical aesthetics, we can see how Rwanda's commemorative practices animate the tensions between the discursive memory—political memory that encapsulates the genocidaires—and the sensible that locates colonial violence in both the past and the present. Commemoration aesthetics meets these hermeneutical challenges in the return to the sensibility that is formed in relation to the commemorative arts themselves, and how they relate to the context of post-genocide discourse. Commemoration is not only social but also political, and it raises questions about the role of what is discursively sensible and how that relates to the community in the way that it intersects with the social development within the context of a history of political violence.

In the following section I will argue that these challenges are cast anew in reference to the Kigali and the Murambi Genocide Memorial Centres. Both types of commemoration, I argue, are sites of massacre, but they present extremely different hermeneutical challenges for understanding the political consequences of the aesthetics of post-genocide commemoration in Rwanda.

THE COMMEMORATION AESTHETICS OF SITES OF MASSACRE

Commemoration appears at the intersections of politics and art, history and colonialism, and within the discursive limits of discourse and the sensible. In Rwanda, the form of commemoration is essential to understanding the larger aesthetic relations of the memorials to their context, just as much as the content or the way in which the genocide is portrayed: whether the memorial creates the space for memory, or displays it through a series of images, or creates a narrative, or negates the space of memory altogether.[10] The question that intertwines history and genocide is the question of what is sensed and what remains as part of the present. Herbert Hirsch argued that it is through commemoration that societies regain hope and learn from mass atrocities.[11] But in either case, commemorations are intended to mean something concrete, and real for the post-genocide.

In "Never Again: Genocide Memorials in Rwanda," Pat Caplan points out that in Rwanda memorials there is distinction between the traditional memorials that narrate the events of the genocide along the lines of the state-driven narrative and those that are composed out of the sites of massacre. The former type of memorial links the images and events of the Rwandan genocide to a narrative form, telling the stories of the victims of violence. She argues that "In most societies where violent conflict has taken place, a prerequisite for healing and reconciliation is the finding of bodies, the mourning of the dead and their burial or reburial preferably by relatives."[12] Memorials, therefore, form a discursive practice of witnessing the violences of the past and put in place a theory of dissent of which they represent an initial reshaping of the experience of the memory in the present.[13]

Rwanda's commemoration aesthetics are distinctly important for contemporary Rwanda, its specific way of addressing genocide and what it means to Rwanda's post-genocide. They also serve as a model for any analysis of cultural reconciliation after the extremes of political violence globally. As the country was determined to face up to their history of genocide through the public use of memory, several types of commemoration were developed. Although Rwanda's commemorations have gained international attention for the striking use of memorial culture to facilitate the process of reconciliation and as a tool that displaces the genocide-denying narratives that began soon after the massacres, they also remain open to questioning what memory means in the post-genocide.[14] What is the role of the sense of political experience of these memorials? What do they say about the social framework in which they enter into and reproduce the work of memory, of shared memory or a shared sense of the past, of recognition, and of community in post-genocide Rwanda? Both questions are tied to *sites of massacre*, and how these spaces have been converted in the memory spaces or into *sites of commemoration*.

These memorials are significant in how they are locations of political violence, on the one hand, and social practices of commemoration, on the other. The *site* is significant in how it determines or sets out its relation to that violence, but it is the site that is specific to the relation of commemoration. In this way, sites of massacre make concrete the use of memory, but it can only do this meaningfully if it speaks from the site of violence, and with the people affected by it. In this sense, geographically, Kigali is important because it is often regarded as the city where the genocide began. The establishment of the Kigali Genocide Memorial Centre, therefore, works to reoccupy the spaces of the origin of the genocide, and to never forget that this is part of the location. It achieves three things: first it provides a type of resistance to genocide deniers. Second, it educates the generations that do not have a sense of the genocide. Third, it makes use of memory to inform or shape an experience of the sense of genocide through its narrative. The Centre emphasizes the role of memory and education as ways of addressing the trauma and culture of Rwanda after the genocide, while also educating non-Rwandans at the same time. Like many Holocaust memorials, it also produces a narrative-structure throughout the displays as a form of memory itself.[15]

Although by all measures the Kigali Centre is effective and culturally meaningful, the museum can only represent the general form of genocide memory through the narratives and images it collects, and in its occupation of space, of Kigali. Sorado writes, "The Kigali Centre's elaborate plans reflect the current global need to create memorial museums that do more than solemnly remember the past, instead using genocide for education and prevention on a national and international scale."[16] If the sense of genocide commemoration is not only about the past, or the recognition of a history, but a continual and contemporary renewal of a search for meaning within what and how one recognizes and tarries with the past and its violence, then in what way does the Centre achieve a meaningful relation as post-genocide when the Centre can only make sensible a past, narrated as a national history? How is this achievement, not simply part of the consumer culture industry surrounding genocides themselves? And further: In what ways does the aesthetic of the Centre actually only make the political experience one that is subjectively important to the spectator or the select group, but animates a sense of the difference between then and now? The Kigali Centre narrates and represents memory relative to state-driven narratives. It holds the narratives of past as past, and thus operates as a closed window within the present. Even though the Kigali Center functions as both a memorial and a source of global genocide education, it does this by also not functioning as a site of commemoration; rather it only functions as a site of state-driven narration.

If the Kigali Centre is part of a memory culture that is prone to be overdetermined by the discursive memory of the political, then the Murambi Genocide Memorial Centre seem to play off of a sense that makes just such an approach problematic. Much like Moses's notion of a form of non-consoling commemoration, the Murambi Centre is particularly disturbing and moves against a narration of the past. The Murambi Centre, which was formerly, the Murambi Technical School, retains memory as site of massacre, and is distinctly not a museum. It is the site that was originally the campus of a technical school and became a site of genocide because it was where Tutsi and others asylum seekers were led to believe that they would receive sanctuary. It is the site where the asylum seekers were slaughtered, their bodies dumped into mass graves or left to rot in the open—and this scene remains as both memory and present.[17] This form of commemoration is not a museum or center, but the conversion of the site of the campus where children and adults were slaughtered into the memorial itself by preserving the people and space as it was and as it remains. Without collapsing into representation or narrative, one tarries not only with the memory but also its present and the present itself is found in the sense, a sensibility of what remains, what has been done, and what is not finished. The entire commemoration is conditioned by the context of the space of commemoration, by the social and cultural importance of the place, and collectivity of being there, with the dead—and therefore *with* the political violence of the genocide as a problem of state violence.

What is made sensible is not narrative, but the traces of violence on the bodies of the victims and in the places of the community. It is important that the commemoration *is not* a representation or display; it is not a narrative or story that does the work of the memorial. Rather, it *is* the bodies of approximately 1,000 children and adults were exhumed from the mass grave that are the site of memory. The memorial presents the killings in a moment and a place of terror, as bodies that bear the marks of the machete, severed limb and life. The scene of the genocide is present in that the school is no longer a school and the people are bodies but no longer people. However, the political violence of the site remains in a particular and aesthetic sense. The sensibility that develops within this site calls into question the present's relation to the memory of death and the present's absence as part of the sense of space and place.[18] Yet, in this context it seems equally important to emphasize that it is the memorial's ability to give a sense of singularity to the atrocities one encounters, to give form to the singularity of mass violence, and the totality of even a single death, on a massive scale, that draws our sense toward a meaning of the political that also retains the violence as a sensibility within the present.

Sites of massacre are marked by a memorializing that remains spatially present in the sense of memorializing of the actual bodies. Without narrative, its temporal arrangement of memory is contradictory within the way bodies, both individually and collectively, are part of the place. In this place, it is making sensible the *time of violence* as past within a present sense of political violence.

What is profoundly present in the sites of massacre is not the spatiality of the memorial, but its relational space-time. It is time without consolation; a sensibility of time that does not make sense of its time. And yet, at the same time, what the sensibility of commemoration shows is that the temporality of political violence is inseparable from the place, and is one that cannot be loosened from the present or made sense of as *only* a memory of a political event of the past. Furthermore, the spatialization of post-genocide memory is precisely a cover for the political experience of the post-genocide itself, since everyone lives this space individually, and the experience remains subjectively located in relation to space. Yet, it is only through a collectivity of violence that these resettle the spaces they occupy. Mass death is visual concrete, yet conceptually abstract.

What hermeneutical aesthetics warrants us to question in Rwanda's commemoration discourse is what not determines the limits of a context of the recognition genocidal violence, but what complications are evaded in the discourse itself. Despite the discursive use of memory as a shared experience, the aesthetics of these sites of commemoration is, therefore, not addressed to the individual, but to an abstract collective.

MOURNING AND THE LIMITS OF REMEMBRANCE

Rwanda's post-genocide memorial culture is unlike any other. The space and forum to mourn publicly is a powerful expression and move toward reconciliation. In acknowledgement of this, commemoration in Rwanda is not restricted to only independent memorials, but also intertwined with public mourning. April 7 through the 13, marks the beginning of the period of National Mourning, which is carried on until the beginning of July. This time begins with large-scale ceremonies and plays are performed to honor the memory of the victims of the genocide, allowing the general public to mourn with the survivors. Significantly, the plays acknowledge that mourning is a social need. Unlike the sites of massacre that require an individual experience with the memorial site, Rwanda's National Mourning Plays rely upon a *public form* of recognition of the sense of the genocide's violence as part of the nation's past. This form of recognition is achieved in many ways, including through large public gatherings and elaborate performances, marking the shift from the aesthetics of memory to practices of mourning. Furthermore, the overarching theme of the performances take on the mood of hope and reconciliation as a projected result of this form of mourning. On one level, National Mourning Plays are grand, choreographed performances depicting the genocide. On another level, they display an overload of artistic expression through a combination of acting, poetry, song, dance, and political speeches. While the scenes do tell stories from the genocide, what is striking is that they do not attempt to capture the memory of the genocide, so much as they aim at recreating *a sense of genocide and commemoration.*

National Mourning is approached as a concrete form of public recognition, and a sign that the government is committed to remembering genocide for the betterment of the society. However, in this context, genocide commemoration cannot be taken up uncritically. In "A Time of Mourning," Rachel Ibreck argues that, "Commemorations are judged to be among the most divisive of state polices: they have been described as 'state violence' and an 'enforced memory' which helps nurture ethnic enmities."[19] Yet, no one argues that commemoration is unnecessary. This suggests that the problem is not simply one that can be captured at the discursive level of politics, but is complicated at the sensible level concerning the meaning of politics within the post-genocide. Ibreck states, "In post-genocide Rwanda the government has used memory to constitute its vision of political community, but has also faced limitations in this endeavor."[20] Ibreck's analysis of the commemoration is important because it situates these rituals and ceremonies within the context of the post-genocide, and surveys the multiplicity of political implications of them.

Rwanda's National Mourning commemoration requires that everybody participates in some way. Ibreck writes, "Commemoration requires interaction, not just attendance, creating opportunities to challenge the dominant public memory. Large crowds attend ceremonies. While some attend in mourning and [out of] a commitment to the dead, others come because they have felt pressured by the government."[21] Beyond the active attending of the events, there is a sense of attending, of being in, or at attention. Moreover, the time of National Mourning is a time of directly being focused on the memory of the genocide, and this is a social and political condition of post-genocide reconciliation.

Who participates and what this means is complicated. The ceremonies are focused on the survivor testimonies, on the sense of mourning from the standpoint of the witness. After all, these plays are also performed in spaces where the language of *Hutu* and *Tutsi* can be invoked in speeches by government officials, which is to say that these terms are used in this period. The words recognize the sense in which Tutsi are victims and Hutu are perpetrators, and therefore, they recognize the sense in which their ethnic divisions were conditions for the possibility of the genocide itself. These plays are performed as discursive history, and these public events are increasingly also the space for young people to gather and participate in these events as a way of engaging in political activism.[22]

What is hermeneutically interesting in these events, then, is that the political experience of the post-genocide practice of mourning appears as National Mourning in two discursive senses. First, mourning is a form of bearing witness to the past of political violence. All spectators are involved, but they are only as witnesses to a political and discursive past. Second, mourning is a way of participating in the present by responding to a public showing and knowing of the past. But beyond the discursive elements, the plays make sensible the present in relation to the past in a particular sense. They establish a post-genocide sensibility that bears the responsibility of the present, on the one hand, and a post-genocide body that bears witness to the political violence of the past, on the other.

Amanda Breed points out that the theater provides the space where perpetrators and victims can weave new relationships, but that it is in these times and through these performances that the body is shot through with anxieties.[23] Likewise, Ibreck writes, "While some participants are provoked to tears and distressed as survivors recount their testimony, others appear to be transported back to the moment of the genocide and begin crying or trying to flee."[24] Indeed, the sense of fear and violence is paradoxically thick during the time of mourning, where actual violence and threats against survivors and the presence of genocide ideology increases.[25] In addition, Ibreck points out that "Rwandans, and not just survivors, may feel heightened anxiety and become very sensitive to the behavior of other people they meet."[26] The *sense of mourning* that follows from these practices remains in question, because mourning remains a question not of *what* or *how* this practice relates to the past as much as it is of *who* it requires to participate and *what* this participation makes senseless.

The sense of mourning is one that is in question in the National Mourning Plays precisely because it is something that is actively constructing the interpretation of memory, publicly, and because it constitutes the aesthetic horizon of Rwanda's post-genocide politics. Although these plays are explicitly talked about as important forms of reconciliation, it is this same sensibility that also traumatizes people with the production of this sense of memory as well—and it is this double sense that needs to be called into question as a permanent state of Rwanda's post-genocide commemoration. The National Mourning Plays frequently cause people to faint or break out in hysterics as they provoke traumatic memories, because they relate or link the present to a making sense not only of memory but of political violence as well. Some people are clearly affected because of the memories evoked, but the ceremonies also reproduce, in a visceral way, the violence of the genocide itself. As Breed writes, "there is the danger that repeating slogans and the government rhetoric of reconciliation will not develop truthful and analytic ways to address the problems facing post-genocide Rwanda."[27] But this is all national performance of memory that builds a phantasmagoria of the post-genocide in memorial practices.

The practice of using public memory and mourning to animate a sense of genocide in post-genocide Rwanda not only is traumatic but also underscores a practice of making former state-sponsored violence present at the aesthetic level, while casting it into the past, discursively. Susanne Buckley-Zistel has pointed out that within this context, while the importance of remembering the genocide is ubiquitous, a form of selective amnesia is also frequent.[28] She argues that such an amnesia must be thought of as part of the coping and working through of the trauma of the genocide, but also as a way of living within the present context of a post-genocide society. The forgetting she describes is also a type of contextualizing that is against the determinism of state-driven memory, and here I think it is appropriate to connect this with not only past trauma but also the work of mourning within the post-genocide. Moreover, the overarching theme of the time of mourning is distinctly one of unity and reconciliation and thus the plays appear to indicate a larger arrangement of the sensible toward this political end. Ibreck problematizes the notion that unity and reconciliation are the only outcomes of this form of commemoration; she sees in these gatherings a type of spontaneous recapitulation of the political at play. She argues that it is important to understand that the time of mourning is the time where the survivor, and those affected by the genocide most, are given public forum and attention. She argues further that, "Commemoration gives survivors a unique opportunity to speak. Their testimonies, alongside the reburials, are the focal point of the ceremonies. Survivors communicate the magnitude of the violations and their enduring consequences. They demand justice; action against genocide denial and an end to the attacks on survivors."[29] Within this context, survivors are given a forum to speak directly against their past and present government and more importantly to form a sense of community and political power that is off limits from the nation-state. Further within the scope of the political, she argues that commemoration functions as opportunities for social contestation and further negotiation to emerge.[30] In all of this, Ibreck's point is apt, politically and culturally. But her analysis shows distinctly the aesthetic difference that is embedded in post-genocide mourning.

While culturally and politically consistent, mourning conceals a conflict over who, what, and when memory can be invoked and what, how, and why government, community and agency can be deployed or restricted as post-genocide violence. These all emerge within the post-genocide as a way of displacing the colonial context through which the genocide was possible. Genocidal violence did not come from nowhere; it was not cultural or political before it was part of the aesthetics of the colonial situation, colonial and postcolonial failures of government, colonial and postcolonial failures of the political, aesthetically. The sense of genocide is made to appear even in the multiplicity of responses to the context of commemoration, contained there in the *sense* of what it means to participate, or to make visible the consequences, or make sensible a righting of the wrong of genocide. These are all the wrong *senses*, or more precisely, this indicates that the commemorative is only possible through the political experience of a derangement of the sensible continuous with the post-genocide.

COMMEMORATIVE VIOLENCE OF THE SENSIBLE

I have argued that the discursive memory in the political domain conceals the political experience of the post-genocide within a sensibility that is particular to it. Post-genocide commemoration expresses a derangement of sensible at the same time it is providing a context for remembering its own political violence. What the aesthetic analysis of post-genocide Rwandan mourning plays tell us is precisely that the sense in which a community requires mourning is exactly what does not make sense, aesthetically even if it does discursively—it indicates a derangement of the sensible first and foremost that makes less sense of state violence as political violence. And they do not make sense because the aesthetics of genocidal violence in and through the post-genocide is excessive to discursive addresses. Whether one is Hutu or Tutsi, the *sense* that appears with the *practice* of mourning is problematic then, in that it is a *sense* that makes the community of the post-genocide Rwanda make *less sense*, not more in relation to the lived experience of survivors.

I want to illustrate the questions of commemorative aesthetics of Rwanda's post-genocide through the narrative of a genocide survivor, because, as Jennie Burnet suggests, it is the commemoration itself that reinscribes forms of the public narrative that are at odds with the lived memories of survivors.[31] One survivor, named Seraphine, pointed out that she does not go the National Mourning Plays, because she is Hutu and therefore excluded from memory and mourning. She is Hutu, but her husband was Tutsi and both were victims of the sense of violence of the genocide before and after. Seraphine recounts that one night, after her husband had attended a mandatory meeting, he had not returned home. She discovered that her husband, "had been hit in the head with a spiked club, but he was not dead. My neighbors found him and brought him home."[32] She then describes how the family kept him hid, first in a bedroom, then in a storage room. She writes,

> I explained to the children that they must say their father was dead if anyone asked. As the war continued, I mostly stayed here at the house so that when the Interahamwe and soldiers came I could keep them from finding my husband. One day General—came to the house with a group of soldiers. When he first came, I thought he was just visiting. But it became clear that he was not here for a simple social call—it was late, after all. He brought me here [*she pointed at the floor*]. He told me that I could have sex either willingly or by force—it was up to me.[33]

Although Seraphine hid her husband by consenting to being routinely raped by the soldiers, her memory is not just forgotten, it is made to be evidence of her complicity with the *genocidaires*.

Commemoration or mourning do more than attempt a general recognition of the genocide; they enact forms of violence. It is not just that her particular situation is silenced in in the National Mourning commemoration; it is *dis*-integrated at the level of the sensible. As such, this subject's relation to the political experience of the post-genocide profoundly does not make sense. And yet, what must also be seen here is that the telling of her story makes visible the event and its context in relation to the genocide, while concealing exactly what does not make sense about it: the reproduction of colonial relations to genocidal racialization. This limit to the sensibility of the post-genocide reveals the post-genocide practices of mourning is split between a sensing of the body without its experience as a political mechanism and through the same sense the practice of mourning makes the experience appear without a practice of being embodied within the sense of mourning.

In any of the commemorative forms of memorial to the genocide, Seraphine's experience is not simply erased or ignored or displaced; rather, it is decontextualized. It is only her Hutu-ness that makes sense in the mourning practices of the post-genocide, but as part of the remembering of Hutu as perpetrator, or her as survivor, but only insofar as Hutu's are not survivors. And it does so in a context in which it is not her *ethnic* or *political* identity that is in question.[34] What Seraphine's testimony bears witness to is that National Mourning Plays make sensible a post-genocide memory of *Hutu-bodies*, bodies without identity, present bodies as pasts structure of violence. At the same time, the sense of these bodies is incorporated into these performances as the cause for public mourning. In "I am Rwandan: Unity and Reconciliation in Post-Genocide Rwanda," Laura Blackie and Nikki Hitchcott point out that in the performances, despite their content, the body is already interpolated as individuated *Hutu* or *Tutsi*.[35] The interpolation of the body is one thing, as it may be necessary for the narrative of the genocide. But, this interpolation carries with it a *sense* of violence and thus more is at stake than what or how a performance constructs its narrative. Regardless of role or overarching structure of the performance, the interpolation of the body is already commensurate with the *sense* of genocide memory reproduced within the *practice* of mourning—and as a memory, the aesthetics of mourning is a practice of the post-genocide arrangement of the sensible. The interpolation of the body is not a mere side effect of the art, but rather a reproduction of post-genocide-body that is marked by a sensibility that also carries with it, or more precisely, *is*, a sense of *difference*. The Hutu-body and all that corresponds to it, the post-genocide practices of mourning leave it senseless, or without a sense if they are not understood as perpetrator-bodies. This is not simply about the practices of memory, community, reconciliation, or interpersonal (or intergenerational) healing, but rather about the development of a sensibility of the political as a derangement of the sensible.

The situation of Seraphine can speak to a wide range of dynamics that complicate commemoration. It is violence that is masked in the commemorative, in the memory and co-memory, and the displacement that this enacts. To talk about her situation is to speak of the contextual violence of her situation as something real, rather than something potential. Hermeneutically, her situation shows that the sense of her experience of memory is political.

It's failure to make sense discursively is the context of violence and this context is not abstract or potential; for the sense of the political experience located outside the discursive, contextual violence is real and constant. It is a *verkerte welt* of violence, that is doubled in the context of genocide against the people of Africa and the globally capitalist world, it is horizon of violence without a sense that has been part of the developing world intertwined with anti-black forms of colonialism. Seraphine is not simply a limit to the public discourse, or of the limits of the public imagination, she is a limit to politics in the post-genocide. Seraphine, like so many others, bring to bear the problem of bodies within the problem of memory. Seraphine, like so many others, are the bodies that cannot be brought into the participation with the practice of mourning—although they are necessarily *there* to be witness to it. The *Hutu-body* appears within the memory work of commemoration, within the practices of the sensibility of the post-genocide, but only as perpetrator.[36] *Her* Hutu-body is not negated or silenced, but integrated into a post-genocide practice of mourning only as perpetrator, or disembodied other, an *other* outside of politics, and possibly a question of *another* politics. But the situation remains and what can't be reconciled is precisely what remains, deranged. As Breed writes, "This kind of theatre reflects government-driven information campaigns based on a carefully scripted history. It does not pursue questions concerning multiple narratives, but rather enacts a singular state-driven narrative."[37] The performance transforms the individual experience to be overdetermined by political meanings both within the representation and modes of expression, but also in the bodies that preform these post-genocide productions. They reorganize a sense of the political, bringing it to bear as memory, on the one hand, and a retainer for colonial violence that is embedded in a post-genocide aesthetic.

The post-genocide sensibility, through which the practice of mourning appears as a continuous practice that recognizes the history of the genocide, it is first and foremost a *de*rangement of the sensible, and a form of commemorative violence.[38] The practices of mourning depend upon the sensibility of the Hutu-body so much that these practices cannot simply make the absence of the dead sensible; rather, they lay bare a sense of mourning dependent on a derangement of the sensible, as a sense of the united political community and a sense of continual political violence, at the same time. Indeed, the problem is not that her experience is not accounted for, but that the commemorative discursive arrangement is mobilized against making sense of such experiences as both intelligible and legitimate. What this means and what it results in is a confrontation with formative violence that is a reality that is configured discursively abstract, if not left out altogether.

POST-GENOCIDE COMMEMORATION VIOLENCE

What I described as intrinsic in Rwanda's post-genocide commemorative aesthetics as derangement of the sensible is nothing more than a horizon of commemorative violence. I do not mean to degrade or distract from the good intentions or important cultural value that memorials and commemoration has. But, as Sordano points out, no act of commemoration can be completely devoid of the political horizon through which it operates. She argues, "Memorial museums are at heart political projects. This does not mean that the good intentions are not there or are deliberate facades for more devious political projects. Rather, it appears that memory today, despite all good intentions, continues to support and sustain the dominant narratives of the past as delineated by the existing powers that be and their priorities."[39] Along with Sordano, I have argued that commemoration is indeed more complex, and more complexly rooted in the aesthetics of the political experience of the post-genocide. As such, this traces a ground through which both political and hermeneutical critiques may begin, emerge, and continue as a deep engagement with the sociocultural and political factors of this structure beyond the discursive and rhetorical. It is from this aesthetic horizon of the post-genocide that the violence that structures the present may be grasped, and one can be properly entangled with the active reshaping of the meaning of anti-genocidal practice, and it can be pursued as both outside of politics and another politics itself.

This is important beyond the domain of hermeneutical aesthetics because it challenges us to think the reality of political violence, violence that falls outside of the discursive, and locates a domain of violence present within that outside. Despite the political commitment of the Rwandan government to recognize the violence of the genocide, the critical theme that runs through all of the forms of commemoration is that the contextual violence outside the discursive is political violence in the most concrete sense. It is the everyday realness of violence intertwined with the sensible and embodied. The aesthetic violence, the failures of the sensible described in the commemoration aesthetics of Rwanda, are global. They are in effect in the contradictory aesthetics, at the sensible level, that remembers or commemorates violence against blacks in the United States, Latin America, and across the globe as normative. They constitute the pattern of through which the extremes of political violence can be recognized as problematically past, and yet are presently structuring a present in which they develop and are reproduced, without context, and without sense. It makes no sense to encourage the development of commemoration and yet to problematize them as sites of violence. And yet, this is exactly the hermeneutical questions that arise when the discursive memory of genocide is critiqued at the level of the sensible.

What does the hermeneutical aesthetics of Rwanda's post-genocide commemoration amount to? Rather than recommend or condemn practices of remembrance, I think the hermeneutical analysis of commemoration raises the question of the sense of the political that is intertwined with a form of political violence. It calls into question not only the positive attributes of memory but also what we might call *post-genocide commemorative violence*. It challenges us to think more complexly about the present, and how post-genocide commemorative violence appears within a political horizon where there is no quarter from this violence. Ultimately, I think this leads to a questioning of contextual violence and seeing it less and less abstractly as the violence that endangers the globally black, and as a violence that is continually present as political violence itself.

NOTES

1. Paul Kagame, "Rwanda's President Speaks at Genocide Memorial Ceremony," *Comments Delivered at the Kigali Convention Center, 2019: Remember-Unite-Renew*, https://www.youtube.com/watch?v=p12kPfUDqg8.

2. See Hans-Georg Gadamer, *Truth and Method*, trans. J. Weinsheimer and D. G. Marshall (New York, NY: Continuum, 2004); and *Philosophical Hermeneutics*, trans. D. E. Linge (Berkeley, CA: University of California Press, 2008); also see Jacques Rancière, *Aesthetics and its Discontents*, trans. S. Corcoran (Malden, MA: Polity Press, 2010).

3. Okonda Okolo, "Tradition and Destiny: Horizons of an African Philosophic Hermeneutics," in *African Philosophy: The Essential Readings*, ed. T. Serequaberhan (New York, NY: Paragon Books, 1991); Tsenay Serequaberhan, *The Hermeneutics of African Philosophy: Horizon and Discourse* (New York, NY: Routledge, 2012); Achille Mbembe, *On the Postcolony* (Berkeley, CA: University of California Press, 2001); *Critique of Black Reason*, trans. L. Dubois (Durham, NC: Duke University Press, 2017); *Necropolitics*, trans. S. Corcoran (Durham, NC: Duke University Press, 2019).

4. Moses, "Empire, Colony, Genocide," 3–54, p. 40.

5. Moses, "Conceptual Blockages and Definitional Dilemmas," 7–36, p. 33.

6. A. Dirk Moses, "Genocide and the Terror of History," *Parallax*, 17, (4), 2011, 90–108.

7. Kingsley Chiedu Moghalu, "The 'Final Solution' to the 'Tutsi Problem'" in *Rwanda's Genocide: The Politics of Global Justice* (New York, NY: Palgrave Macmillan, 2005), 8–24.

8. Alexander Hinton, "Savages, Subjects, and Sovereigns: Conjunctions of Modernity, Genocide, Colonialism," in *Empire, Colony, Genocide: Conquest, Occupation, and Subaltern Resistance in World History*, ed. A. D. Moses (New York, NY: Bergham Books, 2008), 440–59, p. 454.

9. Ibid., 445.

10. James Young, *At Memory's Edge: After Images of the Holocaust in Contemporary Art and Architecture* (New Haven, CT: Yale University Press, 2002); and *Sites of Memory: Perspectives on Architecture and Race*, ed. C. E. Barton (New York, NY: Princeton Architectural Press, 2001).

11. Herbert Hirsch, *Genocide and the Politics of Memory: Studying Death to Preserve Life* (Chapel Hill, NC: The University of North Carolina Press, 1995), 35.

12. Pat Caplan, "Never Again: Genocide Memorials in Rwanda," *Anthropology Today*, 23, (1), 2007, 20–22, p. 22.

13. On the complicated notion of reconciliation and commemoration culture, see Elizabeth King, "Memory Controversies in Post-Genocide Rwanda: Implications for Peace-Building," *Genocide Studies and Prevention: An International Journal*, 5, (3), 2010, 293–309; Rachel Ibreck, "International Constructions of National Memory: The Aims and Effects of Foreign Donors' Support for Genocide Remembrance in Rwanda," *Journal of Intervention and Statebuilding*, 7, (2), 2013, 149–69 and her dissertation, *Remembering Humanity: The Politics of Genocide Memorialization in Rwanda*, 2009; Dirk Moses, "Does the Holocaust Reveal or Conceal Other Genocides? The Canadian Museum of Human Rights and Greivable Suffering," in *Hidden Genocides: Power, Knowledge, Memory*, ed. A. Hinton, T. La Ponte, and D. Irvin-Erickson (New Brunswick, NJ: Rutgers University Press, 2014), 21–51.

14. For discussion of the reconciliation process, see Allison Des Forges, "Ending the Genocide," in *Leave None to Tell the Story: Genocide in Rwanda* (New York, NY: Human Rights Watch, 1999), 692–771; Jennie Burnet, "The Injustice of Local Justice: Truth, Reconciliation, and Revenge in Rwanda," in *Genocide Studies and Prevention*, 3, (2), 2008, 173–93; Christopher Taylor, "Rwanda's *Gacaca* Trials: Toward a New Nationalism or Business as Usual?" in *Genocide and Mass Violence: Memory, Symptom, and Recovery*, ed. D. Hinton and A. Hinton (New York, NY: Cambridge University Press, 2015), 301–20.

15. For a critical analysis of Rwanda's genocide memorials with a focus on Kigali, see Rebecca Jinks, "Thinking Comparatively about Genocide Memorialization," *Journal of Genocide Research*, 16, (4), 2014, 423–40. Also see Helene Dumas and Remi Korman, "Espaces de la memoire de genocide des Tutsi," *Afrique Contemporane*, 238, (2), 2011, 11–27.

16. Amy Sodaro, "The Kigali Genocide Memorial Centre: Building a 'Lasting Peace,'" in *Exhibiting Atrocity: Memorial Museums and the Politics of Past Violence* (New Brunswick, NJ: Rutgers University Press, 2018), 84–110, p. 105.

17. Ibid.

18. Jacques Rancière, "Theater of Images," in *Alfredo Jaar: La Politique des Images* (JRP: Ringier/Bilingual Edition, 2008). While Rancière does take up the question of Rwandan memorials, he specifically focuses on Alfred Jaar's first installation of the Rwanda Project, *Signs of Life*. His question is narrower than the present inquiry, but merits consideration. The work, *Signs of Life*, was composed on postcards that were sent to friends, with the message that X is still alive. Rancière argues that the postcards make use of spaces of visibility as a commemorative act that allows the dead to be named, which too seems to be something that interrupts the sensibility of the post-genocide context. Beyond this Rancière's focus on naming leads him to

consider counting, and what it means to be counted as a mode of democracy, which is outside the focus of this project. For discussion of Alfredo Jaar's the Rwanda Project and Rancière's reading of this project, see Moya Loyd's "Whose Name Counts? Rancière on Jaar on Rwanda," *Contemporary Political Theory*, 18, (3), 2019, 311–30.

19. Rachel Ibreck, "A Time of Mourning: The Politics of Commemorating the Tutsi Genocide in Rwanda," in *Public Memory, Public Media, and the Politics of Justice*, ed. Philip Lee and Pradip Ninan Thomas (New York, NY: Palgrave MacMillan, 2012), 98–120, p. 98.

20. Ibid., 99.

21. Ibid., 110.

22. Ibid., 111.

23. Amanda Breed, "Performing the Nation: Theatre in Post-Genocide Rwanda," *TDR: The Drama Review: War and Other Bad Shit*, 52, (1), 2008, 32–50, p. 32.

24. Ibreck, "A Time of Mourning," 112.

25. Ibid., 113.

26. Ibid., 114.

27. Breed, "Performing the Nation," 42.

28. Susanne Buckley-Zistel, "Remembering to Forget: Chosen Amnesia as a Strategy for Local Coexistence in Post-Genocide Rwanda," *Africa: Journal of the International African Institute*, 76, (2), 2006, 131–50.

29. Ibreck, "A Time of Mourning," 107.

30. Ibid., 114–15.

31. Jennie Burnet, "Remembering Genocide: Lived Memory and National Mourning," in *Genocide Lives in Us: Women, Memory, and Silence in Rwanda* (Madison, WI: The University of Wisconsin Press, 2012), 74–109, p. 86.

32. Ibid., 84.

33. Ibid.

34. Erin Baines argues that while the genocide was explicitly aimed at purging the country of Tutsis, women's bodies became central to Hutu gender politics. See Erin Baines, "Body Politics and the Rwandan Crisis," *Third World Quarterly*, 24, (3), 2003, 479–93; Adam Jones, "Gender and Genocide in Rwanda," in *Gendercide and Genocide*, ed. A. Jones (Nashville, TN: Vanderbilt University Press, 2004), 98—137; Sara Brown, *Gender and the Genocide in Rwanda: Women as Rescuers and Perpetrators* (New York, NY: Routledge, 2017).

35. Laura Blackie and Nikki Hitchcott, "I am Rwandan: Unity and Reconciliation in Post-Genocide Rwanda," *Genocide Studies and Prevention: An International Journal*, 12, (1), 2018, 24–37.

36. Breed, "Performing the Nation," 45.

37. Ibid., 35.

38. Nicholas Mirzoeff, "Invisible Again: Rwanda and Representation after Genocide," *African Arts*, 38, (3), 2007, 36–39.

39. Amy Sodaro, "Memorial Museums: Promises and Limits," in *Exhibiting Atrocity: Memorial Museums and the Politics of Past Violence* (New Brunswick, NJ: Rutgers University Press, 2018), 161–84, p. 183.

Chapter 7

Environmental Racism as Genocide
A Case Study of Shell Bluff, Georgia

Milanika S. Turner

Species in the natural world meet extinction when the environment that sustains them is destroyed. The same is true in low-income communities of color. Instead of overt, direct mass killings, environmental hazards are allowed to fester to the detriment of nearby residents. *Environmental racism* is the term for this particular form of genocide, which disadvantages and endangers communities of color all over the world, especially those of African descent, by locating them near harmful substances and facilities. Environmental racism is an assault upon the present and future health of people of color, their environments, and their communities; furthermore, impeding community vitality is included in the legal definition of genocide and condemned under international law. To provide an in-depth description of the processes by which communities of color burdened with environmental hazards have become victims of genocide, a case study approach was used to examine one of the most heavily impacted communities in the nation—Shell Bluff, Georgia—which is contending with an expanding power plant, a former nuclear weapons factory, abnormally high cancer rates, and very little concern or oversight from state or federal government.

The government's (non)response to the hazards in Shell Bluff illustrates tactics of genocide whereby communities are harmed while the impact of environmental hazards is largely ignored or denied by the government. These tactics are outlined in the following sections to explain the processes by which environmental racism functions as genocide in America: (1) downplay of risk and harm through terminology; (2) weakening of environmental justice movements; (3) targeting of an economically distressed community; (4) control of knowledge production; and (5) failure to enforce environmental regulations. Analysis of these tactics is discussed in a subsequent section to lend additional support to the reframing of environmental racism in the United States as government-sanctioned genocide.

DOWNPLAY OF RISK AND HARM THROUGH TERMINOLOGY

First, it is necessary to explicitly define *environmental racism* and explain how this and similar terms impact the understanding and sentiment attached to hazardous conditions. Several terms are used to describe the relationships among environmental hazards, race, ethnicity, and social class, with environmental justice being the broadest. The Environmental Protection Agency (EPA) officially defines environmental justice as "the fair treatment and meaningful involvement of all people regardless of race, color, culture, national origin, income, and educational levels with respect to the development, implementation, and enforcement of protective environmental laws, regulations, and policies."[1] The Environmental Justice Movement put forth its own definition in 1991 as an outcome of the First National People of Color Environmental Leadership Summit; their interpretation of environmental justice included demands for participation, respect, and an end to the production of toxins.

A few related terms are also used in literature and research. Environmental justice is followed in usage by environmental racism, environmental discrimination, and environmental equity/inequity. These terms are often used interchangeably but do contain distinct differences. Liu (2001) differentiated between them in the following manner:

> Environmental racism is a narrow term with race as its core. In contrast, environmental equity and justice can cover a much broader range, including age, culture, ethnicity, gender, socioeconomic status (income), as well as race, although these terms are more often used in the context of race and income. Similarly, environmental discrimination can be broadly used but is often used in terms of race. Environmental racism and discrimination are negative in nature, while environmental equity tends to be neutral. . . . Environmental racism implies both outcome and causes; that is, people of color bear a disproportionate burden of environmental risks and racism is the cause.[2]

Thus, the full meanings of these terms go beyond denotation. Environmental racism is provocative and incendiary and connects environmentalism to civil rights, thus grabbing the attention of people of color.[3] Robert Bullard, considered the father of environmental justice, defined environmental racism as "any policy, practice, or directive (whether intended or unintended) that differentially affects or disadvantages individuals, groups, or communities because of race or color."[4] The concept is further explained in this elaboration by Benjamin Chavis, Jr.:

> Environmental racism is racial discrimination in environmental policymaking. It is racial discrimination in the enforcement of regulations and laws. It is racial discrimination in the deliberate targeting of communities of color for toxic waste disposal and the siting of polluting industries. It is racial discrimination in the official sanctioning of the life-threatening presence of poisons and pollutants in communities of color. And, it is racial discrimination in the history of excluding people from the mainstream environmental groups, decision-making boards, commissions, and regulatory bodies.[5]

What Chavis explained decades ago was environmental racism as genocide. The aforementioned "official sanctioning" alludes to detrimental actions conducted with the government's approval in *the deliberate* targeting of communities of color. Evidence of this targeting is well-documented.

The General Accounting Office's 1983 study discovered a strong relationship between the locations of hazardous dumpsites and the race and socioeconomic status of surrounding communities, especially in the southern United States.[6] Subsequent studies have resulted in similar findings when it comes to treatment, disposal, and storage facilities.[7,8,9] In 1987, the United Church of Christ Commission for Racial Justice, led by Chavis, published a report which linked institutional racism, corporate greed, and environmental hazards; "Toxic Wastes and Race in the United States" found that communities with the most toxic waste sites and facilities around the nation were disproportionately Black.[10] Toxic waste disposal is not random at all. In fact, the process has resulted in minority neighborhoods carrying a greater burden of the costs, regardless of class.[11] This disparity extends to communities' differential access to decision-making and social or political power.[12] Clearly, environmental racism is real as the evidence shows that some groups are more impacted than others by hazards and that threats and health risks are growing even in the present day.[13]

In contrast to the meaning of environmental racism, the connotation of environmental justice is positive and even aspirational.[14] This may explain why the term is so widely favored, especially by the federal government—its usage grew in popularity during the Clinton administration.[15] Moreover, the federal government's sole use of the term "environmental justice" when referring to unequal risk and hazard distribution allows federal agencies and administrators to distance themselves from the consequences of their own actions; it downplays risk and harm, and avoids conversations around federal involvement in the creation of situations they must later remedy. As a result, government agents are not held responsible for their actual role in the genocide of people of color, especially African Americans, by allowing the poisoning of their environments.

Environmental racism and environmental justice can also be understood as two stages of the same issue. If environmental racism is the problem, then environmental justice is the solution. As such, the Environmental Justice Movement is the social movement that arose to secure and protect the right to a healthy environment for all people. Unfortunately, organized action toward the achievement of environmental justice has been blunted over time through the interference of government and industry.

WEAKENING OF ENVIRONMENTAL JUSTICE MOVEMENTS

Scholars and activists usually agree on Warren County, North Carolina, as the birthplace of the Environmental Justice Movement in 1982, when large protests erupted after state officials created a landfill to dispose of contaminants in a predominately African American community with an elevated poverty rate. However, there were several "smaller" events prior to the protests in Warren County that demonstrated growing social unrest, with environmental hazards throughout the country. Chronologically, "some Native American activists and others consider the first environmental justice struggles on the North American continent to have taken place 500 years ago with the initial invasion by Europeans."[16] There were several events in the centuries after this that showed concern for environmentalism, such as those that promoted preservation or conservation.

It wasn't until the mid to late twentieth century that the present environmental movement gained support and momentum.[17] However, this mainstream environmental movement was considered an elitist effort by and for middle- and upper-class whites as it mostly did not include the participation of non-whites or the poor. The tendency of the mainstream movement was "to conceive of the environment as the unspoiled nature that exists outside of, and even in opposition to, the urban areas inhabited by people of color."[18] As one scholar participating in the initial Earth Day in 1970 noted, "for most African-Americans, the issue of environmentalism would appear to be, at best, abstract—and at worst, irrelevant—to the practical conditions of their daily lives."[19]

In contrast, Daniel Faber insisted that the modern environmental justice movement emerged from several other popular political movements: civil rights, occupational health and safety, indigenous lands, environmental health, community-based movements for social and economic justice, human rights, peace and solidarity movements, and immigrant rights.[20] The United Farm Workers of America, who are mostly Mexican-American, began their fight against pesticide poisoning in the workplace in the 1960s, and their struggle continues to the present day. For others, the jump-off point was the 1967 student protests at Texas Southern University after an eight-year-old girl drowned and died in a Houston residential garbage dump. Other advocates claim civil rights activist Dr. Martin Luther King, Jr., as a proponent of the environmental justice movement because he was in Memphis to support a sanitation workers' strike at the time of his assassination in 1968.[21]

Additionally, the civil rights movement garners further credit for "feeding" the environmental justice movement by demonstrating the power of grassroots movements and conferring on African Americans a sense of empowerment through their activist efforts. This was certainly beneficial in the trials that awaited them and other minority groups, as it was a predominantly African American community (84 percent) that led the first national struggle against environmental injustice in Warren County, North Carolina.[22] The movement later gained momentum when environmental issues were directly linked to community well-being in Jesse Jackson's 1984 presidential campaign, in which he "repeatedly raised environmental issues, from the toxic wastes dumped in working-class and minority neighborhoods, to the connections among poverty, institutional violence, and the physical quality of life experienced by minorities and the poor."[23]

In 1994, President Clinton issued Executive Order 12898, "Federal Actions to Address Environmental Justice in Minority Populations and Low-Income Populations." The order was intended to draw federal attention to environmental justice issues to achieve environmental protection for all people. Executive Order 12898 requires federal agencies to identify, research, and address how their actions and facilities may disproportionately affect health or the environments in minority or low-income communities. The signing of Executive Order 12898 is often considered a victory of the environmental justice movement, though its emphasis on research and health studies has created a rift between environmental justice advocates and positivist scientists who have unsuccessfully sought to prove cause-effect relationships.[24]

Though Clinton's administration seemed to make environmental justice a federal priority, it actually employed a "neocommunitarian" strategy of empowering grassroots environmental justice groups, gaining their trust, and then managing them rather than eliminating or redistributing hazards.[25,26] The government's neocommunitarian strategy coincided with the weakening of environmental justice movements by charitable organizations that required grassroots groups to use less radical objectives and practices in order to receive the funding necessary to sustain their efforts.[27]

TARGETING OF AN ECONOMICALLY DISTRESSED COMMUNITY

While the previous two tactics describe broad processes that contribute to the occurrences of genocide on a macro level throughout the nation, the remaining tactics emerged directly from the analysis of a specific case of environmental racism functioning as genocide. The community of Shell Bluff, Georgia, provided a critical contemporary platform from which to conduct this analysis. Shell Bluff, within Burke County, is located centrally on the far eastern Georgia border, about 120 miles from the city of Atlanta. It is home to the Savannah River Plant (a former nuclear bomb plant) and Plant Vogtle, the 3,100-acre site of two nuclear reactors that have been active since 1987 and generate 15 percent of Georgia's electric power through Southern Company.[28] Though it seemingly provides just a small percentage of the state's electricity, Plant Vogtle is the source of the majority of problems for residents of Shell Bluff, greater Burke County, and nearby areas in both Georgia and South Carolina.

The predominantly African American community of Shell Bluff has cancer rates more than 50 percent higher than communities not near reactors, which is one reason the situation there is termed "environmental racism";[29] however, this statistic only relates to the hazards existing in Shell Bluff at the time of study (which included just two nuclear reactors at Plant Vogtle). Early in 2012, the Nuclear Regulatory Commission (NRC) approved licenses for the construction of two additional reactors at the plant. They were projected to become active in 2016 and 2017 and would make Plant Vogtle the only power plant in the nation with four nuclear reactors.[30] Proponents of expansion of Plant Vogtle often cite the use of a greener fuel source and the creation of jobs as two huge benefits. However, this logic is flawed. Though nuclear energy is better for the environment than the nation's current reliance on coal, it is not worth the dangers of producing and storing it when there are other feasible energy sources such as wind or solar energy.

The decision to place two additional nuclear reactors at Plant Vogtle can be traced to the corporate capitalist restructuring process. This includes the same practices that resulted in the disproportionate placement of ecological hazards in working-class and communities of color neighborhoods around the world. Such practices have been criticized as the neoliberal erosion of environmental safeguards necessary for the corporate capital restructuring process. The restructuring of capital allows corporations to lower production costs, thereby maximizing their profits. A common way to do this is to locate (or relocate) operations to already polluted areas, especially in the American South or overseas. Thus, capitalists selectively victimize already marginalized communities that are not expected to mount much political resistance:

In the United States, the less political power a community of people possesses, the fewer resources (time, money, education, and so on) people within have to defend themselves from potential threats; the lower the level of community awareness and mobilization against potential ecological threats; the more likely they are to experience arduous environmental and human health problems at the hands of capital and the state. Only those economically depressed communities burdened by poverty, high unemployment, and a marginal tax base will "choose" to accept hazardous facilities. Such a trade-off is sometimes made because of the potential for job creation, enhanced tax revenues and the provision of social services, and other economic benefits. In contrast, communities with a strong economic base and a high degree of control capacity over the decision-making processes of local government officials and business leaders are better able to block the introduction of environmental hazards.[31]

Southern Company operated two nuclear reactors in Shell Bluff without much oversight or resistance and chose to further burden an already vulnerable African American community with two more nuclear reactors. In doing so, the corporation treated residents as expendable objects that could "be reduced to a few pennies of stock price or be chosen by market forces as the dumping ground for dangerous industrial waste."[32] Thus, the targeting of this particular African American community was calculated as a business maneuver that would encounter minimal local resistance.

The promise of job creation in this economically distressed county may have decreased resistance to the expansion of Plant Vogtle. Building two more reactors served "as a $14 billion capital investment in Georgia and . . . [promised] to bring more than 3,500 construction jobs and more than 800 permanent jobs."[33] George DeLoach, the mayor of Waynesboro (also located in Burke County), felt that two new nuclear reactors was just what the county needed financially and stated, "Because of the economic situation that we're in now, jobs mean more to them than the environment . . . Everybody wants a good job."[34] Even with the two existing reactors, Burke County was still one of the poorest areas in the state and "trading clean energy and jobs for the health of poor Black citizens without investigating the long-term effects fits the definition of environmental racism precisely."[35] Such environmental blackmail has been established in the literature as occurring when environmental controls are marketed as things that would limit or eliminate jobs. Bullard (1990) observed that

> Black workers are especially vulnerable to job blackmail because of the threat of unemployment and their concentration in certain types of occupations. The black workforce remains overrepresented in low-paying, low-skill, high-risk

blue collar and service occupations where there is a more than adequate supply of replacement labor.[36]

The practice of environmental blackmail can occur within a polluting facility or in the greater community, whereby enforcing environmental standards threatens to eliminate local jobs. Without the potential for economic gain through the creation of new jobs, this frustrated community might have erupted in anger over their living conditions and deteriorating environment long ago.

Many residents were afraid to speak out against Southern Company for fear of losing jobs or being blacklisted; one resident reported, "I had rather have the job and have cancer, so my child can move out."[37] The bleak economic situation in Shell Bluff forced individuals to "choose" between financial stability and physical wellness. Staying in Shell Bluff despite the presence of hazards was not a freely made choice; rather, it was determined by location in the socioeconomic class structure, which prevented escape. As Gregory (1971) attested, "The victim of genocide has no choice in the matter. But it is an act of genocide for a government to create the conditions of hopelessness, frustration and despair among a group of people so that they choose suicide as the only available means of escape."[38] Along these lines, creating a situation so desolate that one chooses martyrdom in the hope that his or her child(ren) may escape to a better life is also an act of genocide. Sending one's progeny away so that they may experience healthful living expels a generation of people from their homeland and forcibly transfers the descendants of one community group to another group. As Schell realized, "Acts of extermination, although usually accompanied by slaughter in the present, are assaults upon the future."[39]

The expansion project at Plant Vogtle is already nearly $1 billion dollars over budget due to faults of Southern Company, but it was state ratepayers and US taxpayers who have been and will continue to pay for these errors.[40] Georgia ratepayers have been paying an additional few dollars ($3.73) on their electric bills every month for the proposed expansion; yet, they will not even reap the energy generated from the third and fourth nuclear reactors to be added, as this energy will be sold to Florida.[41] This contributes an additional economic burden to the community of Shell Bluff while they receive little benefit for their suffering.

CONTROL OF KNOWLEDGE PRODUCTION

Though the NRC must initially approve the construction of nuclear reactors, it does not monitor their impact on surrounding communities. Neither the federal government nor Southern Company, which owns Plant Vogtle, have been willing to examine the effects of the nuclear reactors and the former bomb plant superfund site on the health of local residents. There is existing data that shows high levels of toxins and radiation in nearby natural resources. One opponent of Plant Vogtle's expansion was the Blue Ridge Environmental Defense League (BREDL), a multi-state non-profit community organization. BREDL gathered data that showed the harmful emissions from the nuclear and ordnance plants in the air and water, contamination of the Savannah River and downstream drinking water supply, radiation in fish that increases when the fish are cooked, and higher cancer rates in Black men and women within a 50-mile radius of Plant Vogtle.[42] Downstream from Plant Vogtle and the former Savannah River Plant, few fish are found in the abnormally warm water; fish that are caught in the river have sores on their bodies, and even the pine trees look diseased.[43] Toxic water affects humans and animals directly and indirectly through consumption.

With all of these observations and data, Shell Bluff residents and community organizations have not explicitly rejected the plant's expansion; rather they pleaded with the government to halt the expansion of the plant until an in-depth study of the health risks of living near nuclear reactors is complete. The government's failure to conduct such research demonstrates how those with the most influence in government and industry have the power to produce knowledge by defining harm and risk, deciding who and what should be evaluated, and establishing rules for what should be reported.

Community members in Shell Bluff and surrounding Burke County towns have noticed a difference in how they and other communities are treated when it comes to environmental risks. Residents claim that no one has come to check on them since the plant was built in 1987. Initially, households within ten miles of the reactors were given radios so that they could be notified of an accident at Plant Vogtle; these radios are now nearly thirty years old and have never been replaced.[44] Outspoken residents have compared their treatment with those of similar communities such as Dothan, Alabama, where residents are surveyed annually to assess their health.[45] The concerns of Shell Bluff residents, as well as the residents themselves, seem to have been disregarded despite the numerous environmental safeguards written into federal legislation.

FAILURE TO ENFORCE ENVIRONMENTAL REGULATIONS

One would think it is the responsibility of the EPA to ensure that communities and environments are not overexposed to toxins; however, its power and scope are limited. Since its formation in 1970, the EPA has been given a variety of environmental protection tasks, but its priorities and practices shift with each presidential administration and the dominant political party. The Obama administration's emphasis on nuclear power stymied the situation in Shell Bluff to some extent. In 2010, President Obama announced that Southern Company, the Fortune 500 corporation leading the consortium of utility companies that are building the reactors, would receive over eight million dollars in loan guarantees from the US Department of Energy to build the additional two nuclear reactors at Plant Vogtle.[46, 47]

The NRC's approval of the licenses to build the two new reactors at Plant Vogtle in 2012 are the first such approvals in over thirty years.[48] Many have wondered how and why the licenses were approved, with the nuclear disaster at Fukushima Daiichi (Japan) so fresh in international memory. The NRC decision came less than a year after the tragedy in Japan, an event that continues to wreak global havoc. Though nuclear energy is a greener source than burning coal, neither Southern Company nor the NRC is willing to monitor the resulting radiation levels or impact of the plant on air, water, soil, or health in nearby communities. Aside from the alleged oversight of power plants by the NRC, the EPA is tasked with regulating and monitoring environmental concerns through federal legislation and amendments.

The Federal Water Pollution Control Act (1972) aimed to prevent and eliminate pollution in navigable waterways, as well as create and maintain a water quality that was swimmable and fishable and that could sustain marine and wildlife.[49] Plant Vogtle, as well as the community of Shell Bluff, are situated along the Savannah River. It is the fourth most toxic waterway in the nation and is no longer fishable; while nearby residents do not fish the river for fear of pollution, the nearby Waynesboro community relies on groundwater from wells for bathing and drinking water.[50] Aside from concerns about current pollutants and toxicity levels of the local water, residents fear what will happen to the water supply when two additional nuclear reactors are built in their community.

The Comprehensive Environmental Response Compensation and Liability Act (1986) was created with accountability in mind. It aimed to determine who was responsible for creating toxic or hazardous sites in order to make them responsible for remediation. However, the NRC allows nuclear power plants to monitor themselves. They claim that Plant Vogtle is safe. The research presented by BREDL demonstrates that by insisting Plant Vogtle is safe, the NRC has downplayed the risk and harm stemming from the nuclear plant. In 2011, CNN reporters discovered that very limited independent environmental monitoring was conducted around the reactors because the federal government had allocated zero funds to the state of Georgia to do so.[51] Since this discovery, the Department of Energy agreed to once again allocate money to the state of Georgia for independent environmental testing, but the money would be officially designated to monitor the superfund located across from Plant Vogtle and not the nuclear plant directly.[52]

Finally, the Resource Conservation and Recovery Act (1976) was designed to better manage solid and hazardous waste by regulating its transportation, handling, storage, and disposal. Ideally, violators are pursued by the US Department of Justice and are subject to criminal sanctions and penalties.[53] When it comes to nuclear waste, however, there is still no plan in place to properly dispose of it. As a result, the nation continues to build nuclear reactors and house their waste on site until a better location can be determined to "safely" dispose of it. This means that in Shell Bluff, the hazardous waste as well as the issues resulting from proximity to it grow with each passing day. One such issue is the relationship among toxins, disasters, and environmental racism. According to scholarly literature, chemical accidents have been more likely to occur in areas that are disproportionately African American or low income.[54, 55,56] Grave concern should be given to such findings when considered alongside the knowledge that there will soon be four active nuclear reactors in Shell Bluff.

On the surface, these acts of legislation seem to be equitable actions taken with no specific human group or community in mind. However, environmental racism becomes evident with regard to if and how this legislation is enforced, and if and how violators are penalized. While the EPA is tasked with regulating risks, actions taken in the last century show little more than the management and unequal distribution of environmental risk and harm. African American communities such as Shell Bluff experience further unequal treatment when it comes to monitoring hazards, compensating losses, and remediation of hazardous sites. For example, "white communities see faster action, better results and stiffer penalties than communities where blacks, Hispanics and other minorities live . . . whether the community is wealthy or poor."[57]

By cooperating with polluting industries through the selective, weak enforcement of established environmental safeguards, the United States government is guilty (at the very least) of being a conspirator in the genocide that results from contaminating the air, land, and water in communities of color. The United States, which enacted a social contract as well as legislation to ensure the protection and well-being of citizens, has over time allowed social and environmental protections to deteriorate in favor of corporate and political interests. Neoliberalism, the philosophy of market-led economics, has eroded environmental protection and regulation by allowing polluting industries to influence federal and state action/inaction around environmental issues to serve their own interests. Polluting corporations achieved this by heavily financing anti-environmental organizations, think tanks, research centers, policy institutes, and pro-business political candidates that have weakened both the enforcement of regulations and the remediation of environmental hazards, as seen in the case of Shell Bluff. Thus, environmental racism resulting from governmental policies and practices seems particularly insidious and has been characterized as genocide.

ENVIRONMENTAL RACISM AS GENOCIDE

Several themes have emerged from the analysis of conditions in Shell Bluff, which help in understanding how environmental racism functions as a modern form of genocide; however, these themes are more appropriately classified as the tactics government and industry use cooperatively to commit environmental racism, and thus genocide among communities of color in the United States.

With the first tactic, knowledge of environmental hazards and their impact is shaped (and limited) through control of relevant terminology; not only does related government language serve to minimize risk and harm, but it also allows federal and state agents responsible for safeguarding the environment to distance themselves from the direct consequences of their actions on human life and health. Avoidance of the terms "environmental racism" and "genocide" occurs despite strong evidence that African American communities are deliberately targeted for both toxic waste disposal and the siting of polluting industries. Knowledge is further shaped by controlling the production of research as federal agencies ultimately decide how and if health, risk, and harm are evaluated. Next, grassroots groups which organize to oppose environmental racism find their organizations managed and weakened through cooperation with federal agencies that require them to restrict their activities to receive funding and support.

Furthermore, the economically distressed community of Shell Bluff was targeted for expansion of the nuclear power plant as a result of corporate capital restructuring carried out through environmental blackmail. Southern Company was permitted to assert its "right to profit" over basic and global human rights. Federal and state governments further allowed a percentage of the polluter's financial costs to be shifted onto ratepayers and taxpayers.

Large corporations' control of government has historically weakened protections for the environment, and subsequently people, especially the most vulnerable populations. Hence, the final tactic employed in this genocide was the failure of the federal government to enforce environmental laws and regulations. With various interest groups competing for EPA attention and action, industry has been the most influential and effective. Not only were the residents of Shell Bluff marginalized and their concerns disregarded, but evidence demonstrated that protecting the interests of the corporate and political elite was also of paramount concern.

Thus far, the discussion of environmental racism has only considered human victims. However, the impact is much, much larger. The term "victim" ordinarily refers to persons, and occasionally to animals, but there are other creatures and things that suffer from destructive environmental actions such as plants, fish, and other organisms, in addition to losses of lands, forests, waterways, history, and culture. Naturally, survival depends on the interrelationships among various species. Environmental racism has demonstrated the power to destroy individuals and communities both in whole and in part. When the health and welfare compromised is that of people of African descent, environmental racism shifts from being merely a burden to becoming a subtle form of genocide.

Closely examining the case of Shell Bluff illuminated a pattern of genocide specific to Blacks in America, whereby incidents have moved away from overt acts of violence to become covert, racist assaults embedded into the very structure and governance of the nation. Such a shift requires that contemporary discussions of genocide also evolve to reframe these assaults as both near and current. Thus, genocide no longer occurs only in distant lands and times; it is happening here in America in the present day. As with other genocides, deliberate physical, mental, and economic harm is inflicted upon African Americans in situations of environmental racism. Altogether, the physical, environmental, and financial harm in Shell Bluff amount to structural violence at the hands of the federal government and qualify environmental racism in this African American community as genocide with a government seal of approval.

NOTES

1. Environmental Protection Agency, *Vocabulary Catalog List Detail—Environmental Justice Key Terms*, June 10, 2010, Accessed at: http://ofmpub.epa.gov/sor_internet/registry/termreg/searchandretrieve/glossariesandkeywordlists/search.do?details=&glossaryName=Env%20Justice%20Key%20Terms.

2. Feng Liu, *Environmental Justice Analysis: Theories, Methods, and Practice* (Washington, DC: Lewis Publishers, 2001), 13.

3. Ibid.

4. Ronald G. Burns, Michael J. Lynch, and Paul Stretesky, *Environmental Law, Crime, and Justice* (New York, NY: LFB Scholarly Publishers, 2008), 181.

5. Benjamin F. Chavis, Jr., forward in Robert D. Bullard, *Confronting Environmental Racism: Voices from the Grassroots* (Cambridge, MA: South End Press, 1993), 3.

6. Robert D. Bullard, *Dumping in Dixie: Race, Class, and Environmental Quality* (Boulder, CO: Westview Press, 1990).

7. Commission for Racial Justice, *Toxic Wastes and Race in the United States: A National Report on the Racial and Socio-Economic Characteristics with Hazardous Waste Sites* (New York, NY: United Church of Christ, 1987).

8. Vicki Been, "Locally Undesirable Land Uses in Minority Neighborhoods: Disproportionate Siting or Market Dynamics?" *Yale Law Journal*, 103, (6), 1994, 1383–11.

9. Eric J. Krieg, "A Socio-Historical Interpretation of Toxic Waste Sites," *The American Journal of Economics and Sociology*, 54, 1995, 1–14.

10. Manning Marable, *Black Liberation in Conservative America* (Boston, MA: South End Press, 1997).

11. Bullard, *Dumping in Dixie*, 35.

12. Ibid.

13. Hannah Holmes, *The Secret Life of Dust: From the Cosmos to the Kitchen Counter, the Big Consequences of Little Things* (New York, NY: John Wiley & Sons, Inc., 2001).

14. Luke W. Cole and Sheila R. Foster, *From the Ground Up: Environmental Racism and the Rise of the Environmental Justice Movement* (New York, NY: New York University Press, 2001).

15. Liu, *Environmental Justice Analysis*, 13.

16. Cole and Foster, *From the Ground Up*, 20.

17. Ronald G. Burns and Michael J. Lynch, *The Sourcebook on Environmental Crime* (New York, NY: LFB Scholarly Publishing LLC, 2004).

18. Michael Bennett, "Cities in the New Millennium: Environmental Justice, the Spatialization of Race, and Combating Anti-Urbanism," *Journal of African American Studies*, 8, (1), 2004, 126–41.

19. Marable, *Black Liberation*.

20. Daniel Faber, *Capitalizing on Environmental Injustice: The Polluter-Industrial Complex in the Age of Globalization* (Lanham, MD: Rowman & Littlefield, 2008), 6.

21. See Cole and Foster, *From the Ground Up*.

22. See Bullard, *Dumping in Dixie*.

23. Marable, *Black Liberation*, 240.

24. See Liu, *Environmental Justice Analysis*.

25. Ryan Holifield, "Neoliberalism and Environmental Justice in the United States Environmental Protection Agency: Translating Policy into Managerial Practice in Hazardous Waste Remediation," *Geoforum*, 35, (3), 2004, 285–97.

26. For a well-documented discussion of these federal participatory schemes that have ultimately drained environmental justice movements of political power and energy, see Pellow and Brulle (2005). Also see Piven and Cloward (1977) who observed that historically when elites perceive an uncontrollable insurgency they respond by cultivating lower-class organizations into dependence which results in either the organization's demise when it is no longer of use or its persistence when it is subservient to elite interests, p. xxii.

27. Ryan Holifield, Michael Porter, and Gordon Walker, "Introduction Spaces of Environmental Justice: Frameworks for Critical Engagement," *Antipode*, 41, (4), 2009, 598.

28. Chris Saunders and Lauren Frohne, "Nuclear Power in Georgia: A Closer Look at Plant Vogtle," *Energy Trends Insider*, June 9, 2010, Accessed at: http://www.consumerenergyreport.com/2010/06/09/nuclear-power-in-georgia-a-closer-look-at-plant-vogtle/.

29. Adriane Harden, "Environmental Racism in Shell Bluff, Georgia," *People's Tribune*, 39, (5), 2012, 12.

30. Saunders and Frohne, "Nuclear Power in Georgia."

31. Faber, *Capitalizing on Environmental Injustice*, 25.

32. Gary Cohen, "Toward a Spirituality based on Justice and Ecology," *Social Policy*, 26, (3), 1996, 6.

33. Saunders and Frohne, "Nuclear Power in Georgia."

34. Ibid.

35. Harden, "Environmental Racism in Shell Bluff," 12.

36. Bullard, *Dumping in Dixie*, 10.

37. Matthew C. Cardinale, "Shell Bluff Residents Speak Out on Nuclear Reactors," *Atlanta Progressive News*, January 13, 2012, Accessed at: http://atlantaprogressivenews.com/2012/01/13/shell-bluff-residents-speak-out-on-nuclear-reactors/.

38. Dick Gregory, "My answer to Genocide," *Ebony*, October 1, 1971, 70.

39. Jonathan Schell, "Genesis in Reverse," *Bulletin of the Atomic Scientists*, 63, (1), 2007, 28.

40. JoAnn Merrigan, "Environmental Groups: Plant Vogtle Reactors Almost One Billion over Budget," *WSAV News*, 3, May 15, 2012, Accessed at: http://www2.wsav.com/news/2012/may/15/environmental-groups-plant-vogtle-reactors-almost--ar-3797937/.

41. Cardinale, "Shell Bluff Residents."

42. Blue Ridge Environmental Defense League, *Why We Oppose the Expansion of Plant Vogtle*, Last modified July 21, 2010, Accessed at: http://www.bredl.org/pdf2/Vogtle_Factsheet100721.pdf.

43. Cardinale, "Shell Bluff Residents."

44. Ibid.

45. Ibid.

46. Steve Hargreaves, "First New Nuclear Reactors OK'd in over 30 Years," *CNNMoney*, February, 2012, Accessed at: http://money.cnn.com/2012/02/09/news/economy/nuclear_reactors/index.htm.

47. Saunders and Frohne, "Nuclear Power in Georgia."

48. Hargreaves, "First New Nuclear."

49. Burns and Lynch, *The Sourcebook*.

50. Harden, "Environmental Racism in Shell Bluff," 12.

51. Cable News Network (CNN), "Plant Vogtle," *Broadcast*, 2011, Accessed at: http://www.youtube.com/watch?v=P6f-e-vyzlc&feature=player_embedded.

52. Ibid.

53. Burns and Lynch, *The Sourcebook*.

54. Paul B. Stretesky and Michael J. Lynch, "Environmental Justice and the Prediction of Distance to Accidental Chemical Releases in Hillsborough County, Florida," *Social Science Quarterly* 80, (4), 1999, 830–46.

55. Daniel D. Derezinski, Michael G. Lacy, and Paul B. Stretesky, "Chemical Accidents in the United States, 1990–1996," *Social Science Quarterly*, 84, (1), 2003, 122–43.

56. M. R. Elliott et al., "Environmental Justice: Frequency and Severity of U.S. Chemical Industry Accidents and the Socioeconomic Status of Surrounding Communities," *Journal of Epidemiology and Community Health*, 58, (1), 2004, 24–30.

57. Marianne Lavelle and Marcia Coyle, "Unequal Protection: The Racial Divide in Environmental Law," *National Law Journal*, 15, (3), 1992, 51–52.

Index

Achebe, Chinua, 31
aesthetics, commemoration, 79–83
Africa, 55–60, 75; European colonization, 56, 58; genocide as normative practice, 57–60; mass deaths, 56; political economy, 56; premature death, 56
Africa Contingency Operations Training and Assistance (ACOTA), 69
African Americans: civil rights movement, 99; environmental racism and, 100–107; hazards monitoring and, 56. *See also* slavery
African Union (AU), 32, 55, 69–70
African Union Mission in Somalia (AMISOM), 69
Alexander, Michelle, 47
Aly, Götz, 46
Amin, Idi, 29
Angelus Novus (Klee), 34
anti-Black violence, 39–40; genocidal structure of, 47–53. *See also* slavery
aphorism, 2
Arendt, Hannah, 45, 48
art for healing, 24
Arusha Peace and Reconciliation Agreement, 60–61, 62, 65, 66, 67, 71
Atlantic slave trade, 41, 47

Auschwitz Death Camp Art at Northeastern Illinois University, 15
Axis Rule in Occupied Europe (Lemkin), xiii

Bauer, Yehuda, 40, 43, 45, 46–47
Belgium, 1, 14
Benjamin, Walter, 34
Black Earth (Snyder), 46
Blackie, Laura, 88
Black Lives Matter, xiv, 39
Blood, Archer, 10n9
Blue Ridge Environmental Defense League (BREDL), 103
Breed, Amanda, 85, 89
Buckley-Zistel, Susanne, 85
Bullard, Robert, 96–97, 101–2
Burnet, Jennie, 87
Burundi, 55–71; colonization, 14; as constitutional monarchy, 3; East African Community (EAC) and, 70–71; economic insecurity, 63–65; electoral democracy, 66; genocidal politics in, 60–63; geopolitics, 68–69; history, 1; impunity, 65–68; independence, 1, 14; liberal peace, 68; Ndadaye's assassination, 7, 8, 60; peacekeeping missions, 68–69; population, 14; regional fallout, 6–7;

regional non-intervention in, 69–71; versus Rwanda, 3–4; as a success story, 61
Burundi genocide of 1972, 13–24; continuing relevance, 7–9; as planned massacre of Hutu elites, 13; public acknowledgement, 8; survivor's account, 15–24
Burundi National Defense Force, 69
Buyoya, Pierre, 7

capitalists, 100–101
Caplan, Pat, 79
Card, Claudia, xii, 41, 48
Catholic Commission for Justice and Peace in Zimbabwe, 28, 30
Catholicism, 61
Chavis, Benjamin, Jr., 97
chemical accidents, 105
Chrétien, Jean-Pierre, 10n14
Civil Rights Council (CRC), xiii–xiv, 49–50
civil rights movement, 99
Clinton, Bill, 99
CNDD/FDD, 61, 62, 65, 67, 69, 71
CNN, 104
collective amnesia, 8–9
colonialism, x, xiii
commemoration in Rwanda, 75–91; aesthetics, 79–83; colonialism and, 77–79; genocide discourse and, 76–79; interpretive problems of, 77; sites of massacre, 79–83
commemorative violence, 86–91. See also mourning
community organizations, 103
complementary enemies, 1
Comprehensive Environmental Response Compensation and Liability Act, 104
"Conceptual Blockages and Definitional Dilemmas in the 'Racial Century': Genocide of Indigenous Peoples and the Holocaust" (Moses), 43–44
"Conceptual Constraints on Thinking about Genocide" (Moshman), 43

Congo, xi
contextual violence, 88–89
Convention on the Prevention and Punishment of Genocide, 27
criminalization of Black life, 51
Criminal Justice system of United States, 50
critical theory, 76

Davidowitz, Lucy, 45
DeLoach, George, 101
Department of Corrections (DOC), 52
Desroches, Christian, 10n13
Disarmament Demobilization and Reintegration (DDR), 62
Dupaquier, Jean-Francois, 10n14
DuVernay, Ava, 50

East African Community (EAC), 70–71
economic insecurity, 63–65
Entumbane uprisings, 29
environmental blackmail, 102
environmental discrimination, 96
environmental justice: civil rights movement, 99; defined, 96; environmental racism and, 96–98; movements, weakening of, 98–99; neocommunitarian strategy, 99
Environmental Protection Agency (EPA), 96, 103–6
environmental racism, 95–107; case of Shell Bluff, 100–107; concept, 95, 96–97; environmental justice versus, 97–98
European and African Union summit, 32
European colonial rule, 78
Executive Order 12898, 99

Faber, Daniel, 98
false twins, 3. See also Burundi; Rwanda
Federal Water Pollution Control Act, 104
First Chimurenga, Zimbabwe, 31
First National People of Color Environmental Leadership Summit, 96

Index

Floyd, George, 39, 53

Gadamer, Hans-Georg, 76
General Accounting Office, 97
Geneva Convention on Genocide, 57–58
genocidal violence, 56, 59
genocide, ix; concept, xii–xiii, 27; ideology of, 58; as normative state practice, 57–60
genocide discourse, ix–x, 76–79. *See also* commemoration in Rwanda
Genocide Watch, 27–28
Ghana, 32
Gukurahundi massacres, 27–32, 34, 35; casualties, 30; Genocide Watch on, 27–28; historical background, 29–30

Harroy, Jean-Paul, 4
hermeneutical aesthetics, 76
Hinton, Alexander, 78
history: historical materialist view, 34; production of, 34
Hitchcott, Nikki, 88
Hitler, 46
Hitler's Beneficiaries (Aly), 46
Holocaust, 40; American slavery *versus*, 44–47; political imaginary and, 40–44; pragmatic dimensions of, 46–47; as a singular event, 40; suffering, 44–47
Holocaust memorials, 80
Hotel Rwanda, 15
Hoyt, Michael, 5, 9n10, 10n11
human rights abuses, 8, 28, 32
human rights groups, 67–68
Hutton, Patrick, 34
Hutu, 13, 16–17, 22–24; Belgian authorities and, 3; peasant revolt and, 4; social revolution, 4. *See also* Burundi; Burundi genocide; Rwanda
Hutu-body, 88–89

Ibreck, Rachel, 83–86
ikiza, 1, 15, 20, 21, 22
International Criminal Court (ICC), 66

Jackson, Jesse, 99
James, Joy, 40
Jews, 43
Jim Crow, 41, 47, 49–50, 53

Kagame, Paul, 75
Katz, Steven T., 45
Khumalo clan, 29
Kigali Genocide Memorial Centre, 80–81
King, Martin Luther, Jr., 99
Kissinger, Henry, 6
Klee, Paul, 34
Krueger, Kathleen Tobin, 10n17
Krueger, Robert, 10n17
Kuper, Leo, 27
kwihutura, 14

League of Nations Mandates, 3
Legal Resources Foundation, 28
"Le génocide de 1972 au Burundi: Les Silences de l'Histoire" (Lemarchand), 13
Lemarchand, René, 13, 14
Lemkin, Raphaël, xii–xiii
Levene, Mark, ix
liberal peace, 68
Liu, Feng, 96
Löwy, Michael, 35

Marshall Plan, 56
mass incarceration, 47
mass killing. *See* genocide
Mbembe, Achille, 76
memory: *Angelus Novus* (Klee), 34
Merkel, Angela, 32
Moghalu, Kingsley Chiedu, 78
Moses, Dirk, x, 42–43, 77
Moshman, David, 43
mourning: limits of remembrance, 83–86; sense/sensibility, 85–89; survivor's account, 87–89
movements of mass violence, 34
Mugabe, Robert, 28–32; anti-imperialist rhetoric, 30–33; assassination attempt on, 29–30; European and African

Union summit, 32; Ncube on, 30; North Korea and, 30
Murambi Genocide Memorial Centre, 81
Murambi Technical School, 81
Mutua, Makau, 56

Namibia, 57
National Mourning/National Mourning Plays, 83–85
Native Americans, 44
Nazi genocide. *See* Holocaust
Ncube, Pius, 30
Ndadaye, Melchior, 7, 8, 60
Ndayishimiye, Evariste, 55, 67
Ndebele, 29
Ndlovu-Gatsheni, Sabelo J., 32–33, 60
neocommunitarian strategy, 99
neoliberalism, 105–6
The New York Times, 32
Nixon, Richard, 6
Nkala, Enos, 29
Nkomo, Joshua, 31
Nkurunziza, Pierre, 7, 8, 55, 61–65, 67, 70
North Korea, 30
Ntare, 5
nuclear disaster at Fukushima Daiichi (Japan), 104
nuclear reactors in Shell Bluff, 100–105
Nuclear Regulatory Commission (NRC), 100, 102, 104
Nyamitwe, Alain, 8

Oaskarsson, Gunilla Nyberg, 10n19
Okolo, Okonda, 76
Omer, Ibrahim, 14
On the Concept of History (Benjamin), 34
Organization of African Unity (OAU), 31–32, 69
The Origins of Totalitarianism (Arendt), 48
orphans of genocide, 1

Party for Hulu Emancipation (*Parti de l'Emancipation du Peuple Hutu*), 4
Patterson, Orlando, xii, 48

Pax Europaea, 57
peacekeeping missions, 68–69
penal system of the United States, 51–53. *See also* prisoners in the United States
Pentecostal Church, 8, 10n19
phenomenology, 76
Plant Vogtle, 100–105
political leadership, 58
political violence, xiii
post-conflict societies, 56
Power, Samantha, 2
pragmatic *versus* non-pragmatic genocide, 44
prisoners in the United States, 51–53; genocidal practices and, 52–53; medical care and, 52; punitive decisions and, 52

regional non-intervention in Burundi, 69–71
Resisting State Violence: Radicalism, Gender, and Race in U.S. Culture (James), 40
Resource Conservation and Recovery Act, 105
Rieff, David, 8–9, 33–34
Rwagasore, Louis, 58
Rwanda, xi–xii, 2, 14, 15, 55, 70, 75–91; Belgian rule, 3; Burundi compared with, 3–4; civil war, 7; Clinton's decision, 2; colonization, 14; commemoration, and mourning, 75–91; Hutu asylum, 7; independence, 3; press coverage of genocide, 1
Rwanda's Genocide (Moghalu), 78
Rwandese National Union (*Union Nationale Rwandaise*), 4

Santayana, George, 2
Savannah River, 103, 104
Savannah River Plant, 100, 103
Second Chimurenga, Zimbabwe, 31
selective genocide, 5, 10n9
Serequeberhan, Tsenay, 76

Shell Bluff, Georgia, 100–107; African Americans, 100; community organizations, 103; nuclear reactors, 100–105; Plant Vogtle, 100–105; Savannah River Plant, 100, 103; tactics of genocide, 95–96
Shona, 28, 29
silence, 13
sites of massacre, 79–83. *See also* commemoration in Rwanda
slavery, 39, 41–42; as an American institution, 47–51; corporal punishment to slaves, 50–51; as a cultural genocide, 42–43; economy of, 50; exclusion from genocide studies, 41, 43; Holocaust *versus*, 44–47; plantation owners and, 49; as political atrocity, 41; political imaginary, 43; suffering, 44–47
social death, xii, 41, 48, 52, 53
South African Peace and Reconciliation Agreement, 66
Southern Company, 100–104, 106. *See also* Plant Vogtle
Speight, Jeremy, 62
state violence, x, xiii, xiv, xv, 47, 83; as criminal violence, 39
Stockholm International Peace Research Institute (SIPRI), 69
Straus, Scott, 58, 67
student protests at Texas Southern University, 99

Texas Southern University, student protests at, 99
Third Chimurenga, Zimbabwe, 31–32
Thirteen Amendment to the US Constitution, 50, 53
thoughtlessness, 45–46
"A Time of Mourning" (Ibreck), 83
toxic waste disposal, 97
"Toxic Wastes and Race in the United States," 97
Truth and Reconciliation Commission and Special Tribunal, 55–56, 62, 65

Tutsi, 14, 21; elitism of, 14; refugees fled to Burundi, 4. *See also* Burundi; Burundi genocide; Rwanda
tutsification, 14
Twa, 14

Uganda, xi
UN Human Rights Commission, 55, 58
United Church of Christ Commission for Racial Justice, 97
United Nations (UN), 55
United Nations Convention on the Prevention and Punishment of the Crime of Genocide, xiii
United States: as a conspirator, 105; Executive Order 12898, 99; penal system and prisoners, 51–53; *We Charge Genocide* petition, xiii–xiv
University of Bujumbura, 4
UN Trusteeship Council, 3
US Department of Energy, 104–5
US Department of Justice, 105

victim, 107

Wade, Abdoulaye, 32
We Charge Genocide petition, xiii–xiv
Wittig, Katrin, 62
Wolpe, Howard, 10n17

Zimbabwe, xi, 27–35; Entumbane uprisings, 29; First Chimurenga, 31; independence, 28, 29; Second Chimurenga, 31; Third Chimurenga, 31–32
Zimbabwe African National Liberation Army (ZANLA), 29
Zimbabwe African National Union – Patriotic Front (ZANU-PF), 29
Zimbabwe African People's Union (ZAPU), 29
Zimbabwe People's Revolutionary Army (ZIPRA), 29
Zulu, 29

List of Contributors

Patricia Daley is associate professor in human geography, Oxford University. She is also an Official Fellow and Geography Tutor at Jesus College, Oxford. She has commented on the 2015 political violence on Burundi on Al Jazeera and the BBC World Service. She is also author of *Gender and Genocide in Burundi: The Search for Spaces of Peace in the Great Lakes Region* (2008) and co-editor of the Routledge Handbook on South-South Relations (2019).

Chielozona Eze is associate professor of English and postcolonial studies at Northeastern Illinois University, Chicago Illinois. His main research concerns ethics and empathy through poetry and literature. He is author of *The Dilemma of Ethnic Identity: Alain Locke's Vision of Trans-Cultural Societies* (2005), *Postcolonial Imagination and Moral Representations in African Literature and Culture* (2011), and *Ethics and Human Rights in Anglophone African Women's Literature: Feminist Empathy* (2016).

Alfred Frankowski is associate professor in the Department of Philosophy at Southern Illinois University, Carbondale Illinois. His research is in nineteenth- and twentieth-century European philosophy, aesthetics, critical race theory, and post-colonialism. He is author of *The Post-Racial Limits of Memorialization: Toward a Political Philosophy of Mourning* (2015).

René Lemarchand is professor emeritus of Political Science at the University of Florida. His research has shaped critical studies in genocide in Africa. His books include *Political Awakening in the Belgian Congo* (1964), *Rwanda and Burundi* (1970), *Selective Genocide in Burundi* (1974), *Burundi: Ethnocide as Discourse and Practice* (1994), and *The Dynamics of Violence in Central Africa* (2009).

Jeanine Ntihirageza is associate professor at Northeastern Illinois University, and Department Chair of Anthropology, English Language Program (ELP), Philosophy, and Teaching English to Speakers of Other Languages (TESOL). Her current research interests are in linguistics, teaching English as a second language, teaching about Africa and genocide in Africa and the African diaspora.

Lissa Skitolsky is the Simon and Riva Spatz Visiting Chair, Department of Jewish Studies and associate professor of philosophy, Dalhousie University. She is a human rights advocate for the women at the State Correctional Institution as Muncy, Pennsylvania. Her research focus is in feminist philosophy, genocide studies, twentieth-century continental philosophy, and political philosophy. She is currently working on a book exploring hip-hop as genocide testimonial.

Milanika S. Turner is assistant professor of sociology at Florida Agricultural and Mechanical University. Her research interests are in environmental justice, cultural anthropology, criminal justice, and urban sociology. She has experience consulting several projects funded by organizations such as the U.S. Department of Homeland Security's National Center of Excellence for the study of Preparedness and Catastrophic Event Response (PACER) and the National Organization of Black Law Enforcement Executives (NOBLE).